R.E.A.D.Y.
for Inclusion

Teacher Tested Tools That Work
for Students with Autism
and Other Disabilities!

Kandis Lighthall, M.A.

Autism and Behavior Training Associates

*"Helping you to find the keys to
unlock the potential of students
on the Autism Spectrum"*

ABTA Publications
Redding, CA USA

Autism & Behavior Training Associates
ABTA Publications and Products
PO Box 492123
Redding, CA 96049

For information on ordering this manual or on workshops provided by Autism & Behavior Training Associates on this and other topics, please see our websites at:

www.autismandbehavior.com

www.abtaproducts.com

R.E.A.D.Y. for Inclusion

ISBN 978-0-9761517-6-0
Copyright © 2007 Autism & Behavior Training Associates
All rights reserved.
Revised © 2009 Kandis Lighthall, M.A.

Cover Design and photo by Mary A. Livingston

Printed in U.S.A.
Book manufacturing services provided by
Red Tail Custom Book Manufacturing
www.redtail.com

TABLE OF CONTENTS

DEDICATION

Janet Susan Holland
1953 – 1997

Janet, my life long friend taught me many valuable lessons about life and all the possibilities it holds. Janet and I lived inclusion as we grew up together, she with the challenges of Down Syndrome and me with the typical challenges of growing up. Janet demonstrated to me that friendship is based on mutual appreciation and how important it is to look inside for the true essences of a person. I know that Janet's influence molded my career and has made me a better person. Although Janet is gone, her spirit continues to light my path and I am very thankful for her continued influence.

ACKNOWLEDGEMENTS

As I refine and expand this manual, I must again acknowledge my friend and colleague, Patty Schetter, who had the original vision to combine all the individual tools that I had developed to support students in inclusive settings into a step by step process that could help many others systematically address inclusive education. Her enthusiasm for this project has continued and now along with ABTA trainer Victoria Murphy I have been motivated to expand this manual and create a protocol for school districts to follow in preparation for inclusive education.

I continue to be thankful to the many talented professionals that I have had the privilege to work with throughout my career. In the early years, Barbara Walter, my paraprofessional who saw the hidden talents in every student and with me made the community our inclusive classroom. The young high school student, Lauren Frost-Bishop, who volunteered her time making a connection with students with autism, and who now is an itinerant teacher working with students on the autism spectrum in many inclusive settings. These two individuals and many others, too numerous to name, have been part of the wonderful team of people that must be recognized for their contributions to my growth and the lives of the students in their care.

My deepest appreciation continues to go to the many families that I have had the honor to work with over the years. Your passion and advocacy for your children has inspired me to do a better job answering the tough questions you have posed. I am humbled by your strength and only hope that my efforts have helped you reach your goals for your children.

Last, but never least, I thank my family Jeff, Sara, and Bryce whose support and encouragement have made all the difference. I could not be the person I am without each of you.

PREFACE

This book is the result of my many years working as a classroom teacher and a Program Specialist for students with disabilities. For the last decade my sole focus has been working with students who have an Autism Spectrum Disorder. Working in special education is very rewarding, but also very challenging at times. The rewards come from the working with wonderful students who bring talents and gifts to the classroom; families who are passionate about working to help their child be the best he or she can be; and the many dedicated professionals who want to make a difference in the lives of others. One of the challenges over the years has been the lack of tools to assess for unique needs in specific situations, especially in inclusive education. Because of this lack, teachers and other professionals have created tools that have worked for them, but often these tools are never distributed to others who could benefit from a tool that works.

This manual has been developed over my career in public education. Although I have taught in the general education classroom, the majority of my career has been spent teaching and supporting students who experience significant challenges with learning and behavior. It has always been my philosophy that students with differing abilities can successfully learn together in a general education setting when given the appropriate supports and instruction. The big question I always asked myself is, "How do I know what is needed to support learners in the least restrictive environment of the general education classroom?"

Each chapter in this manual is the result of my attempts, over many years, to answer this question. Every time that I thought I had the full answer, another question would be asked. Even now as I rewrite the original *R.E.A.D.Y for Inclusion* I have additions to make. This manual has evolved into a protocol that may be used in two ways. First, the manual may be used in a school for a specific student as it was originally designed, and secondly as a tool for system change within a school district.

It has always been exciting to create something that works and makes a difference for the students and staffs I have worked with, but it is even more exciting to pull all the tools together and pass them on to other professionals and parents. It has been my life's mission to make a difference and it is my hope that this revised manual of *R.E.A.D.Y for Inclusion* will do just that for parents and professionals who share the common goal of preparing all students to be productive community members.

INTRODUCTION

Since the passage of Education for All Handicapped Children Act (PL 94-142) educators and parents have needed to develop methods and strategies to support students with disabilities in the least restrictive environment (LRE). While LRE is defined as a continuum, the first consideration for LRE is the age-appropriate general education classroom. This LRE placement may be for part or all of the day, with supports and services as outlined in the student's Individual Education Plan (IEP).

The purpose of this manual is to address the need of educational teams to develop appropriate least restrictive environments in general education settings. The manual provides systematic and quantifiable tools which will allow educational teams to evaluate their own philosophy, environments, individual student needs, as well as, individual staff and peer support.

The scope of this manual accomplishes what the title says. It helps both school districts and individual educational teams get "ready" to "include" or place a student with special needs on a school campus and/or in a general education classroom. It is often a lack of "readiness" that results in frustration for administrators, educators, parents, and most of all, the students. Careful planning and preparation is critical when placing a student with a disability in the least restrictive environment or "inclusive" setting. Frequently only an observational assessment is used to prepare for the inclusive placement. This manual offers educators informal tools to quantifiably evaluate inclusive settings and supports. Although all these tools were originally developed for students with an Autism Spectrum Disorder they have been proven effective with student who have other disabilities.

This manual begins in Chapter 1 by providing the reader with a protocol for developing a shared vision between school staff. It is very important that the school community share the same understanding of least restrictive environments and all that "inclusion" entails. Activities and suggestions for staff awareness are discussed.

The following five chapters address the acronym R.E.A.D.Y. from the title. Chapter 2 addresses the R. by providing a tool to evaluate the "readiness" of the student with disabilities to participate as a student in the inclusive setting. This tool asks what skills require additional instruction, accommodations and/ or modifications for successful participation as a student. It also offers instructional strategies and curricular suggestions.

The E. stands for the "environment" for instruction. Chapter 3 presents a checklist called the V.E.S.T. to evaluate the "environment" for instruction. The acronym represents the four areas that are necessary for optimizing learning for students with Autism Spectrum Disorders and other related attention and learning disabilities. General education teachers report that by systematically addressing these ecological factors, students with other learning differences such as ADD and ADHD have demonstrated improvements in their abilities to attend and participate in instruction.

In Chapter 4 A. explains "accommodating" for academic and learning difference. Accommodations and modifications are a required part of the Individual Education Plan (IEP). There is often confusion over the definition of these terms, as well as how the use of accommodations and modifications affect the expected outcome for the student who is included in the general education setting. This chapter provides the reader with a checklist that clarifies questions an IEP team might have. It also supports general and special education teacher collaboration and provides a common view of the student's needs for the IEP team.

The D. which is covered in Chapter 5 stands for "determining" levels of support for the student who is included. Often the student's increased need for support is interpreted as requiring an additional adult in the classroom or a 1:1 aide. Chapter 5 outlines a 3 step procedure that may be used to determine the specific areas of need and when the support is required. This in-depth analysis provides an educational team with an evaluation tool that systematically answers the questions surrounding a request for additional adult support.

Chapter 6 covers the Y. or "your" natural peer supports. As the research reveals, the classroom peers can be a resource and support to students who are included. The research also notes that with specific training and awareness of the student who is included, the typical peer can assist in teaching both social and academic skills. This chapter discusses a strategy to develop awareness and the foundation for friendship.

The reader may use the chapters in this manual as stand alone tools to address specific questions in the inclusive setting or they may move through the manual in a linear fashion. However, it is recommended that the protocol outlined in Chapter 1 be the foundation that a school uses to develop solid groundwork, as they get "R.E.A.D.Y" for inclusion. Experience tells us that inclusive education requires a team approach for optimal success, thus it is always best to develop a shared vision on a school campus from the very beginning.

CHAPTER 1

GETTING R.E.A.D.Y.
FOR INCLUSION WITH A SHARED VISION

The first shared vision of inclusive education was introduced in 1975 with passage of the Education for All Handicapped Children Act (PL 94-142). This law delineated procedural safeguards and the rights of children with disabilities and their families to receive a free and appropriate public education (FAPE) in the least restrictive environment (LRE), or what is currently known as an inclusive setting. The reauthorization of PL 94-142 in 1990 with (PL 101-476) the Individual with Disabilities Education Act (IDEA) initiated the civil rights movement for students with disabilities and increased the vision of LRE with an even greater focus on the inclusion of students with disabilities in general education settings. In 2004 IDEA was again reauthorized refining and expanding on the existing law.

The implementation of these laws has created challenges to school systems across the nation. School systems had many questions to answer and found that there was not always a clear answer. The following answers to frequently asked questions may be of assistance to school sites and districts that are beginning a systematic process of addressing inclusive education.

What is the general vision of a good education for all students? There is not a generic answer to this question. The

1

answer is based on the personal perspectives and values held by parents, students, teachers, and the community. As a country we have set forth laws that ensure that every individual has the right to an education that is equitable. A common shared vision of a good education is result oriented. Typically it is felt that a student has had a good education if the student has acquired the skills to be able to function as a contributing member of society after finishing his or her course of study. Once again, one's personal perspective of a contributing member of society influences standards of success.

What is the vision of a good school? This is a question that has been researched to determine key qualities that are present in a good school. It is interesting to note that high test scores are not frequently mentioned in the lists of characteristics. The qualities identified by professionals and students may be categorized in three areas: people, the environment, and attitudes.

The important people in a good school include an administrator who provides strong leadership. Administrative leadership was reported in a study of teacher's impressions to be either the greatest support or the greatest obstacle to successful inclusive education (Trump and Hange 1996). The next key people are the teachers who see each and every student as a learner. The final people who make a school good are the parents who are invited to collaborate with the educational staff. Parents complete the team of people who all share a common focus which is the education of children.

The school environment must be a place where students,

staff, and parents feel safe. The environment should also be structured and well organized, yet offer flexibility to meet individual teaching and learning needs.

The prevailing attitude of a good school is one of acceptance of individual learning styles and the belief that all children can learn given the appropriate support and instruction. Individualized social, emotional, and intellectual supports should be available to meet the individual assessed needs of each learner.

Basically a good school is a place where everyone, students, parents, and professional want to be. Each person is valued for their unique talents; diversity is celebrated; and everyone is happy to be living and learning together.

What terms are used by schools when talking about educational services for students with identified disabilities?
The evolutionary movement toward educating all students as one body of children in their neighborhood schools has used various terms over the years. The terms integration, mainstreaming, inclusion, and full inclusion can be used to track the path to what is commonly known today as inclusive education.

In the initial stages of the movement towards inclusive education, schools talked of integrating students with disabilities on a general education school campus. Integration often consisted of physically placing classrooms of students with disabilities on school campuses. In some cases physical integration evolved into opportunities for students to socially integrate at appropriate times, such as lunch, recess, and assemblies. The term integration was abandoned by many due to the connotation that the student with disabilities had been "excluded" from the daily activities of the school community until they were integrated.

Education began to move closer to inclusive education with the concept of mainstreaming. This strategy placed students with disabilities in a general education classroom to participate in a subject where there was a possibility for academic or social success. The mainstreaming concept frequently was implemented without extra supports for the classroom. This often left general education teachers feeling like students with special learning needs had been dumped on them.

For some, the term inclusion connotes the same meaning as integration or mainstreaming, but brings with it identified supports that are necessary to ensure student success in a general education setting. However, there are others who feel that the terms integration, mainstreaming, and inclusion share the underlying feature of implied "exclusion" from the general education setting for some part of the day.

Thus, evolved the term "full inclusion" which has been defined by many as the placement of a student with disabilities in a general education setting 100% of the time with supports and services provided, as identified on the student's IEP. A student is never excluded from a general education setting based on an identified disability label.

It is very important that individual schools and school

districts are aware of the various meaning of these terms. Inconsistent use of these terms may result in miscommunication and misunderstandings that ultimately result in frustration for all.

What is inclusive education? There are many dimensions to inclusive education. It is not a strategy or a placement, but more a philosophy of educating children. As Paula Kluth (2003) states, "Inclusion is more than a set of strategies or practices, it is an educational orientation that embraces differences and values the uniqueness that each learner brings to the classroom." This author agrees with the former statement and would add that most teachers, when given the support to understand the unique learning needs and skill deficits of a learner do a wonderful job teaching the learner with diverse needs. Many general educators have reported that their experience with the student with ASD has helped them grow as an educator. They also have stated that they are now more able to assist other learners who may not have an identified disability, but approach learning differently.

Are all public schools required to include students with disabilities in general education setting? Yes, it is the law. It has been the law for more than thirty years, but it continues to present challenges to educators. Occasionally schools have thought that inclusive education was an option that they could choose to implement; however it is not a choice, it is a legal requirement even if the school does not feel adequately prepared.

An underlying false perception held by some people is that there are two educational systems; one system that serves the "average" student and one system that serves the "special" student. In actuality there is only one educational system to serve all students regardless of their abilities. Special education was created to provide individualized supports and services to students who have been found eligible to receive additional assistance to attain educational benefit. Special education is a set of services and supports not an educational system or "place" where students with disabilities are educated. The perception that there are two educational systems has occasionally set up a paradigm of "our students" and "your students" with clearly defined roles as to who is responsible for which students. Two separate but equal systems of education was not the intent of the law. Inclusive education is the term that is helping to move perceptions back to the philosophy of one educational system. Schools educate children. Special education is only a system of supports and services created to assist the public education system teaching children what they need to learn to become contributing members of society.

Why do schools need a shared vision? A school is a community. As in any community there are visions of how the community will operate and function best to meet the many needs of all the citizens living there. In the school community there are many citizen including the students, parents, para-professionals, and professionals. Each citizen of the school has roles and responsibilities to ensure that the school functions well to meet everyone's needs. The school typically has a vision of how the facility should be maintained, how extracurricular events will occur, how grades are reported, what curricular materials are used, and expected student behavior, just to name a few. When these visions are shared by all citizens of the school, typically the school runs efficiently and the citizens are content and making progress. However, when there is not a shared vision there can be inefficiency which results in discontentment, unrest, and frustration.

Addressing the needs of students who have unique learning styles and/or identified disabilities requires a shared vision. If a school or district has a faulty perception of their responsibilities for educating all students, there may be many consequences from simple frustrations to legal ramifications. Developing a shared vision of how a school and/or district will meet the needs of their entire student population is critical to the effectiveness of the school community.

How do schools develop a shared vision of the education of children in their school community? Developing a shared vision is a systematic process which requires the commitment of some time and a willingness to embrace some new ideas. The main factor that will influence the amount of time it will take to generate a shared vision is the current perceptions of the professionals at the school regarding the education of students with diverse learning styles and identified disabilities. Remembering that the question each person must ask is, "Not who should be included, or not excluded, from a general education setting, but "How can we make the general education environment work for all learners?"

The next section in this chapter will outline simple procedures and protocols to assist professionals in developing a shared vision regarding inclusive education. The following chapters of R.E.A.D.Y. for Inclusion provides educators with practical, field tested, ideas to assist them in preparing for and supporting a student with an Autism Spectrum Disorder (ASD) or other disability in a general education setting. The tools and strategies are based on what research indicates are best or promising practices for working with students with Autism Spectrum Disorders or other learning differences. They are offered to assist school teams in answering the question, "How can I do this?"

Steps to Developing a Shared Vision of Inclusive Education:
The steps listed below in Figure 1.1 are intended to assist a school staff in their initial self reflection and evaluation regarding the topic of Inclusive Education.

6 Steps to a Shared Vision

1. Complete a self evaluation checklist
2. Define terms used at the school site
3. Write a shared vision of Inclusive Education
4. Identify a "Collaboration Team" to communicate with the school parent organization
5. Summarize needs from self evaluation checklist
6. Develop an action plan for support and training based on the self evaluation checklist.

Figure 1.1

The overlapping purpose of these steps is to identify areas of training that would be helpful in increasing teacher skills and confidence when teaching all learners, while developing a shared vision of inclusive education for their school site. Steps 1 – 3 may be completed during one extended meeting time or may be completed at three shorter meetings. The typical time commitment of staff to this project ranges from one hour to several hours. Those staff members who choose to form the "Collaboration Team" will spend more time completing Steps 4 – 6.

Step 1. Complete a Self Evaluation Checklist: This checklist asks educators and administrators to self evaluate their current level of training and personal confidence in areas related to inclusive education. Topic areas include the law, the definition of terms, the impact of specific disabilities on learning, strategies and supports, motivation, collaboration, and facilitating peer support. The checklist includes twenty four items. The staff checks their level of training and confidence across three levels (See Figure 1.2).

The checklist may be completed at several different times. It may be done in private for self reflection; at a staff meeting as a discussion starter; or as the opening activity for steps 2 and 3. Staff completing this checklist should be reassured that the purpose of the checklist is to evaluate individual knowledge and skill level; not to evaluate thier personal skills as an educator or administrator. This information is to be used to identify areas for training and support to increase confidence in teaching students with diverse

R.E.A.D.Y. for Inclusion

INCLUSIVE EDUCATION:
Training & Confidence Self Evaluation

Name (Optional):_____ Position/Grade:_____ Date: _____

The purpose of this checklist is to identify areas for training and support to build confidence when working with students who present differently as learners. Put a (✓) in the box that currently best describes you.

Training Received	Self Evaluation of Confidence
No Training: never had a training	**Low:** Minimal skills or knowledge on topic
Introduction/Overview: have had content training only	**Medium:** Some skills or knowledge on topic
Hands-on training: application of strategies and skills	**High:** Confident implementing and talking about topics

Topic Areas	Training Received			My Level of Confidence		
	No Training	Intro/ Overview	Hands-On	Low	Med	High
1. The law relating to educating students with disabilities						
2. My role as an educator/administrator working with students with different learning styles						
3. My role as an educator/administrator working with students with a disability and an IEP						
4. The definition and practice of integration						
5. The definition and practice of mainstreaming						
6. The definition and practice of inclusion						
7. The definition and practice of full inclusion						
8. The definition and practice of inclusive education						
9. ADD and ADHD and their impact on a student						
10. Autism Spectrum Disorders and their impact on a student						
11. Learning Disabilities and their impact on a student						
12. Emotional Disturbance and the impact on a student						
13. Accommodations: purpose and function for a student						
14. Modifications: purpose and function for a student						
15. Environmental considerations for the classroom						
16. Classroom Organization/Management						
17. Charting pupil progress and data based decision-making for students with an IEP						
18. Utilizing additional adult staff in the classroom						
19. Collaborative planning, teaching, and parent-professional collaboration						
20. Celebrating diverse talents, strengths and interests						
21. Motivating the unmotivated student						
22. Developing peer awareness of unique abilities						
23. Facilitating a network of peer support and friendship						
24. Transition planning specific to your age group						

Additional Comments:

Figure 1.2: This form is found on the CD in the back of this manual. Permission to copy this form for noncommercial educational purposes is granted to the owner of R.E.A.D.Y. for Inclusion.

10

learning styles. A school site may simply choose to use this checklist as a stand alone tool to gather information; or they may choose to quantify the results to more objectively determine their individual needs. The procedures for quantifying the checklist are discussed in Step 5. This process may be done by a self selected "Collaboration Team" or a specialist who is assisting the school site address inclusive education.

Step 2. Definition of Terms Used At the School Site: This is an activity for the entire staff and is the beginning of the development of a "shared vision". When the checklist is used as the introductory activity to Step 2 the staff will already have been introduced to some of the terms they will be asked to define. Typically this activity is led by a facilitator who is a specialist or individual who is well versed in inclusive education and the laws relating to special education.

     Purpose: This activity is to help staff recognize that often there is a misunderstanding of the meaning and implication of the terms used when discussing the education of students with disabilities. Through this activity the staff will generate agreed upon definitions to use consistently among themselves and when talking with parents.

     Procedures for the Activity:
- Divide the participants into small groups of 3-4 people. This can be done in homogeneous grouping according to grade or level (e.g. primary and intermediate); or heterogeneously mixing grades and levels.

- Inform the groups that they will have about 10 minutes to define a list of words as they are used on their school site.

- Have each group select a person to record their definitions and be prepared, as a group, to debrief their definitions in the large group.

- The facilitator may either write the following terms on a chart or hand out a worksheet with the terms listed. The terms are least restrictive environment, integration, mainstreaming, inclusion, full inclusion, and inclusive education.

- During the debriefing the facilitator solicits definitions and records the ideas on a chart paper, concluding with a shared definition. If there is not a shared definition the facilitator may reflect with the staff on what difficulties this confusion might cause for parents and professionals.

- The facilitator should conclude the activity with the historical evolution of the terms as discussed in frequently asked question number three which was discussed earlier in this chapter. Other resources that might be helpful to the facilitator are listed at the end of this chapter.

Time Allotment for Activity: This activity takes approximately 30 to 45 minutes; however this may vary based on the size of the group and the amount of discussion during the debriefing process.

Step 3. Write a Shared Vision of Inclusive Education: This activity may follow directly after Step 2 or it may be facilitated at a different meeting time.

Purpose: This activity allows the participants an opportunity to write their personal definition of inclusive education and gradually build a definition that can be agreed upon by the entire staff.

Procedures for the Activity:

- The facilitator requests each participant to write their personal definition of inclusive education at the top of a piece of paper within a 3-5 minute time frame.

- Next the participants are asked to get into heterogeneous groups (mixed grade levels) of 3 – 4 people to share their definitions and identify words that they have in common. This may take 5 – 7 minutes.

- The groups of 3 – 4 are now asked to double in size or form 2 large groups. Each of these groups will be given a chart paper and asked to write their definition of inclusive education using the words that they had in common. About 10 – 12 minutes may be required.

- Each group will present their definition to the entire group for review and input. This may take 3 – 5 minutes.

- After group input the facilitator requests that the group compose a definition which reflects the consensus of the entire staff. The facilitator will record this definition on a new chart paper. This may require about 5 minutes.

Time Allotment for Activity: This activity takes approximately 35 to 45 minutes; the group size, personal perspectives, and amount of experience and knowledge may increase the amount of time required. Given the total time available the facilitator may choose to spread the activities out over several meeting times.

4. Identify a "Collaboration Team" to Communicate with the School Parent Organization: Research tells us that active parent participation contributes to the characteristics of a good school, thus it is strongly encouraged that the newly developed "shared vision" of inclusive education be shared with the parent group. Some schools have found it helpful to ask a few parent to join the entire staff in the process of developing a shared vision. In that case this step could be omitted.

    Purpose: It is important to seek parent input and support for strong team building; maintaining open communication; and creating a strong sense of community within the school. Not to mention, accessing many gifted and talented parents who can provide insightful perspectives to educators.

    Procedures for Developing a Team:
- Identify the number of professional on the team. A small team of three to five individuals usually is recommended.
- Allowing members to self select participation usually works well because each member has a personal desire to participate.

- It is preferable to have a heterogeneous group that represents different grade levels and expertise.

- Once the team is established they may first choose to meet with the leaders of the school's parent organization and after input from the parents meet with the entire parent group.

Time Allotment for Activity: This will vary according to the type of meeting the team structures. Typically 30 to 45 minutes should be adequate. Once again variables such as group size, personal perspectives, and amount of experience and knowledge may increase the amount of time required.

5. Summarize Needs from Self Evaluation Checklist: This step is required only if the school is choosing to use the information on the Inclusive Education Training and Confidence Self Evaluation Checklist for more than a self evaluation. The summarization may be completed by a specialist or a team of staff members. The checklist maybe summarized with a simple tally method (see Figure 1.3) or may be assigned numerical values to determine a percentage of training received and level of confidence. (See Figure 1.4)

Purpose: Summarizing this checklist assists a school or district in determining topics for future trainings to enhance classroom support. The data may also be used as a pre-post training measure of increased teacher confidence either on an individual teacher basis, or on an overall staff level of confidence.

Procedures for Summarizing Needs and Confidence:

- Each teacher's checklist is reviewed and a tally of each response is summarized on the Summary of Data form (See Figure 1.3).

- The five topic areas that receive the most checkmarks are identified at the bottom of the Summary of Data form ranked from highest to lowest total tallies. If several topics are tied at a ranking note all the topics. The number of the topic may be ranked. When the information is reported back to the staff the full topic should be written out.

- The same procedure is used to summarize the level of teacher confidence. An example of a completed Summary of Data form can be found on Figure 1.3.

The individual teacher responses may also be summarized using a percentage formula. This gives the team a quantifiable measure that may be easily used to demonstrate staff growth in training and confidence. (See Figure 1.4.) The procedure to determine percentage scores is as follows:

- Each "Training Received" level is assigned a point value
  - Hands-On training   = 2
  - Introduction/Overview = 1
  - No Training   = 0
- Each "Level of Confidence" level is assigned a point value
  - High   = 2
  - Medium   = 1
  - Low   = 0

Topic Areas	Training Received			My Level of Confidence		
	No Training	Intro/ Overview	Hands - On	Low	Med	High
1. The law relating to educating students with disabilities	2	12	2	10	6	0
2. My role as an educator/administrator working with students with different learning styles	2	12	2	8	8	0
3. My role as an educator/administrator working with students with a disability and an IEP	2	6	8	8	6	2
4. 4 he definition and practice of integration	6	8	2	12	2	2
5. The definition and practice of mainstreaming	2	8	6	8	6	2
6. The definition and practice of inclusion	6	8	2	10	6	0
7. The definition and practice of full inclusion	7	7	2	14	2	0
8. The definition and practice of inclusive education	10	6	0	16	0	0
9. ADD and ADHD and their impact on a student	4	6	6	8	8	0
10. Autism Spectrum Disorders and their impact on a student	10	2	4	14	2	0
11. Learning Disabilities and their impact on a student	4	8	4	10	6	0
12. Emotional Disturbance and the impact on a student	4	10	2	12	4	0
13. Accommodations: purpose and function for a student	6	4	6	14	2	0
14. Modifications: purpose and function for a student	6	4	6	14	2	0
15. Environmental considerations for the classroom	6	8	2	10	6	0
16. Classroom Organization/Management	4	10	4	8	8	0
17. Charting pupil progress and data based decision-making for students with an IEP	10	4	2	14	2	0
18. Utilizing additional adult staff in the classroom	6	8	2	10	6	0
19. Collaborative planning, teaching, and parent-professional collaboration	6	6	4	10	6	0
20. Celebrating diverse talents, strengths and interests	8	4	4	10	4	2
21. Motivating the unmotivated student	2	8	6	8	8	0
22. Developing peer awareness of unique abilities	6	6	4	10	6	0
23. Facilitating a network of peer support and friendship	10	4	2	8	8	0
24. Transition planning specific to your age group	12	4	0	14	2	0
Total number of tallies divided by the total number or tallies for all 3 columns in Training and Confidence equals the percent of teachers at each level.	141/384= 37%	163/384= 42%	82/384= 21%	260/384= 68%	116/384= 30%	8/384= 2%

Rank the five topic areas receiving the highest number of tallies under the "No Training" column:
1st: #24;   2nd: # 8, 10, 17, 23;   3rd: #20,7   4th: #4, 6, 13, 14, 15,18, 19, 22;   5th: #9, 11, 12,16,12,3,5,21

Rank the five topic areas receiving the highest number of tallies in the "Low" Level of Confidence column:
1st: #8;   2nd: #7, 10, 13, 14,17, 24;   3rd: #4,12;   4th: #1, 6, 11, 15, 18, 19, 20, 22;   5th: #2, 3, 5, 9,16, 23

Figure 1.3: Sample of Summarization of Group completing Training and Confidence Self Evaluation.

- Each column is summarized at the bottom based on the number of points earned. Any checkmark in either the No Training or Low Confidence columns will score no points. Each checkmark in the Introduction/ Overview or Medium column receive a score of one. Thus, if a teacher had eleven checkmarks in these columns they would score eleven points which would be written at the bottom of the column. If the teacher had two checkmarks in either the Hands-On or High Confidence column they would score a four because each checkmark equals two points.

- The scores per column are added together and this is the total score for the teacher (e.g. 11+4=15). To determine the percentage the teacher's total score is divided by 48, which is the total points possible if a teacher marked every topic area as either Hands-On or High, (e.g. 2x24=48). The result shown in the bottom row of Figure1.4 provides an example of this procedure. The teacher's total score in the Training Received column is 15, when this is divided by 48, total possible points, the percentage of training this teacher has received is 31% (e.g. 15 / 48 = 31%). This indicates that the teacher requires approximately 69% more training to build a strong understanding to support inclusive education.

- The same procedure is completed on the Level of Confidence. See Figure 1.4 for an example of an evaluation using percentages.

Step 6. Develop An Action Plan For Support and Training Based On The Self Evaluation Checklist: The summary of data will provide a school site or district a guideline to develop trainings that will be customized to individual needs of their staff.

	Training Received			My Level of Confidence		
Topic Areas	No Training	Intro/ Overview	Hands-On	Low	Med	High
1. The law relating to educating students with disabilities		✓			✓	
2. My role as an educator/administrator working with students with different learning styles		✓			✓	
3. My role as an educator/administrator working with students with a disability and an IEP		✓			✓	
4. The definition and practice of integration		✓			✓	
5. The definition and practice of mainstreaming		✓			✓	
6. The definition and practice of inclusion		✓			✓	
7. The definition and practice of full inclusion		✓			✓	
8. The definition and practice of inclusive education	✓			✓		
9. ADD and ADHD and their impact on a student			✓		✓	
10. Autism Spectrum Disorders and their impact on a student			✓	✓		
11. Learning Disabilities and their impact on a student		✓			✓	
12. Emotional Disturbance and the impact on a student		✓			✓	
13. Accommodations: purpose and function for a student	✓			✓		
14. Modifications: purpose and function for a student	✓			✓		
15. Environmental considerations for the classroom	✓			✓		
16. Classroom Organization/Management	✓			✓		
17. Charting pupil progress and data based decision-making for students with an IEP	✓			✓		
18. Utilizing additional adult staff in the classroom	✓			✓		
19. Collaborative planning, teaching, and parent-professional collaboration	✓			✓		
20. Celebrating diverse talents, strengths and interests	✓				✓	
21. Motivating the unmotivated student		✓			✓	
22. Developing peer awareness of unique abilities		✓			✓	
23. Facilitating a network of peer support and friendship	✓				✓	
24. Transition planning specific to your age group	✓			✓		
Total Scores	0	11	4	0	14	0
Percentage	15/48= 31%			14/48= 29%		

Figure 1.4: Sample of scoring the Training and confidence Self-Evaluation.

19

This summary information should be provided to the entire staff for evaluation and the development of a collaborative plan of action for one to three years. If the school only completed the self evaluation the first action might be to seek a facilitator to present Steps 2 and 3 to lay the foundation to build on with other training.

Professionals and parents must recognize that implementing a successful shift to an inclusive education philosophy does not just occur because it is a desired outcome. As the research reports successful inclusive education takes time, training, planning, and preparation with a team approach. However, a child should never be denied access because a school does not feel fully prepared. The steps outlined in this chapter can give any school a "jump start" in preparing for inclusive education. A team that will be working directly with the student with disabilities may require some initial intensive training and support as a program is initiated. The questions to ask are, "How can we, as a team, solve our problems and make inclusive education a success?"

In summary, including a student with disabilities is not just about placing one student in a general education classroom. It is about the philosophy and training level of the entire school site. Inclusive education systematically addresses the needs of the student, but also requires the support and understanding of the entire school to truly succeed. The following chapters offer many tools and strategies that may be quickly learned and implemented to support a team in developing basic student skills to teach; establishing an appropriate learning environment; identifying accommodations and modifications to address academic needs; and develop adult and peer support.

REFERENCES

Kluth, Paula. *"You're Going to Love This Kid!" Teaching Students with Autism in the Inclusive Classroom.* Baltimore, Maryland: Paul H. Brookes Publishing Co. 2003.

Trump and Hange. *Teacher perceptions of and strategies for inclusion: A regional summary of focus group interview findings.* Charleston, WV: Appalachia Education Laboratory (ERIC Document Reproduction Service No. ED 397-576).

RESOURCES ON INCLUSIVE EDUCATION

Anderson, W., Chitwood, S., and Hayden, D. *Negotiating the Special Education Maze: A Guide for Parents and Teachers.* Bethesda MD: Woodbine House, 1997.

Doyle, M. *The Paraprofessional's Guide to the Inclusive Classroom: Working as a Team.* Baltimore, Maryland: Paul H. Brookes Publishing Co. 1997.

Downing, J. *Including Students with Severe and Multiple Disabilities in Typical Classrooms.* Baltimore, Maryland: Paul H. Brookes Publishing Co. 2002.

Falvey, M. *Inclusive and Heterogeneous Schooling: Assessment, Curriculum, and Instruction.* Baltimore, Maryland: Paul H. Brookes Publishing Co. 1995.

Fisher, D., Sax, C., and Pumpian, I. *Inclusive High Schools: Learning for Contemporary Classrooms.* Baltimore, Maryland: Paul H. Brookes Publishing Co. 1999.

Giangreco, M. Cloninger, C. and Iverson, V. *Choosing Options and Accommodations for Children: A Guide to Planning Inclusive Education.* Baltimore, Maryland: Paul H. Brookes Publishing Co. 1993.

Hammeken, P. A. *The Teacher's Guide to Inclusive Education: 750 Strategies for Success!* Minnetonka, MN: Peytral Publications, 2007.

Jorgenssen, C. *Restructuring High Schools for All Students: Taking Inclusion to the Next Level.* Baltimore, Maryland: Paul H. Brookes Publishing Co. 1998.

Landers, M. and Weaver, H. R. *Inclusive Education: A Process, Not a Placement.* Swampscott, Mass: Watersun Publishing Co. Inc, 1997.

McNary, S., Glasgow, N., and Hicks, C. *What Successful Teachers Do in Inclusive Classrooms: 60 Research-Based Teaching Strategies That Help Special Learners Succeed.* Thousand Oaks, CA: Corwin Press, 2005.

Peterson, M., and Hittie, M. *Inclusive Teaching: Creating Effective Schools of All Learners.* Needham Heights, MA: Allyn & Bacon, 2003.

Putnam, J. W. *Cooperative Learning and Strategies for Inclusion: Celebrating Diversity in the Classroom.* Baltimore Maryland: Paul H. Brookes Publishing Co. 1993.

Sailor, W. (Ed.) *Whole-School Success and Inclusive Education: Building Partnerships for Learning, Achievement, and Accountability.* New York, NY: Teachers College Press, 2002.

Schaffner, C. B. and Buswell, B. E. *Opening Doors: Strategies for Including All Students in Regular Education.* Colorado Springs, CO: PEAK Parent Center, Inc. 1991.

Stainback, S. and Stainback, W. *Curriculum Considerations in Inclusive Classrooms: Facilitating Learning for All Students.* Baltimore Maryland: Paul H. Brookes Publishing Co. 1992.

Stainback, S., Stainback, W. and Forest, M. *Educating All Students in the Mainstream of Regular Education.* Baltimore Maryland: Paul H. Brookes Publishing Co. 1989.

Stainback, W. and Stainback, S. *Support Networks for Inclusive Schooling: Interdependent Integrated Education.* Baltimore Maryland: Paul H. Brookes Publishing Co. 1990.

Thousand, J., Villa, R., and Nevin, A. *Creativity and Collaborative Learning: A Practical Guide to Empowering Students and Teachers.* Baltimore Maryland: Paul H. Brookes Publishing Co. 1994.

University of New Hampshire. *Treasures: A Celebration of Inclusion.* Concord, NH: Office for Training and Educational Innovations, The Institute on Disability/University Affiliated Program, 1993.

University of New Hampshire. *Changes in Latitudes, Changes in Attitudes: The Role of the Inclusion Facilitator.* Concord, NH: Office for Training and Educational Innovations: The Institute on Disability/University Affiliated Program, 1993.

Wood, J. *Adapting Instruction to Accommodate Students in Inclusive Settings.* Upper Saddle River, NJ: Prentice-Hall Inc. 1998.

Yanoff, J. C. *The Classroom Teacher's Inclusion Handbook: Practical Methods for Integrating Students with Special Needs.* Chicago, IL: Arthur Coyle Press, 2000, 2007.

RESOURCES ON
AUTISM SPECTRUM DISORDERS

Attwood, T. *Asperger's Syndrome: A Guide for Parents and Professionals.* London, England: Jessica Kingsley Publishers, 1998.

Bolick, T. *Asperger Syndrome and Adolescence: Helping Preteens and Teens Get Ready for the Real World.* Gloucester, MA: Fair Wind Press, 2001.

Flowers, T. *The Color of Autism: Methods to Reach and Educate Children on the Autism Spectrum*: Arlington TX: Future Horizon, 1999 & 2002.

Grandin, T. *Thinking in Pictures and Other Reports Form My Life With Autism*. New York, NY: Vintage Books, 1995.

Moore, S. *Asperger Syndrome and the Elementary School Experience: Practical Solutions for Academic and Social Difficulties.* Shawnee Mission, KN: Autism Asperger Publishing Co. 2002.

Notbohm, E. *Ten Things Every Child with Autism Wishes You Knew*. Arlington TX: Future Horizon, 2005.

Notbohm, E. *Ten Things Every Student with Autism Wishes You Knew.* Arlington TX: Future Horizon, 2006.

Ozonoff, S., Dawson, D., & McPartland. *A Parent's Guide to Asperger Syndrome & High-Functioning Autism.* New York, NY: The Guilford Press, 2002.

Ozonoff, S., Rogers, S., Hendren, R. *Autism Spectrum Disorders: A Research Review for Practitioners.* Arlington VA: American Psychiatric Publishing Inc. 2003.

Twachtman-Cullen, D. *How to be a Para Pro: A Comprehensive Training Manual for Paraprofessionals.* Higganum, CT: Starfish Specialty Press, 2000.

Twachtman-Cullen, D. & Twachtman-Reilly, J. *How Well Does Your IEP Measure Up?* Higganum, CT: Starfish Specialty Press, 2002.

Wagner, S. *Inclusive Programming for Elementary Students with Autism.* Arlington TX: Future Horizon, 1999.

Wagner, S. *Inclusive Programming for Middle School Students with Autism/Asperger's Syndrome.* Arlington TX: Future Horizon, 2002.

CHAPTER 2

R.E.A.D.Y.
READINESS OF STUDENT BEHAVIOR

Assess for Expected Behavior with the
School Participation Checklist

Who is the School Participation Checklist (SPC) designed for? The SPC was originally developed to assist in preparing to transition preschool students with an Autism Spectrum Disorder (ASD) to a general education setting. However, over time the checklist has been adapted and successfully used with students from kindergarten through 12th grade. There are 3 checklists that are designed to evaluated Preschool to 3rd grade, 4th to 8th grades, and 9th to 12th grades. (See Figures 2.1, 2.2, and 2.3) Each checklist asks the same basic questions but uses wording that is appropriate to each age groups.

School Participation Checklist: Preschool – 3rd Grade

Student: _____ Evaluator: _____ Date: _____

Key: G = generalized; M = mastered; L = learning; N = not ready to learn; ✓ the demonstrated skill level

Activity/Skill/Behavior	G=0	M=1	L=2	N=3	Comment
1. Responds to classroom rules appropriately					
2. Uses appropriate touch to others (peers and adults)					
3. Stays focused on teacher when appropriate					
4. Responds to individual instructions					
5. Responds to group and conditional directions					
6. Typical class routines are followed without cues (puts backpack away, gets in line)					
7. Does not isolate, stays near or with peers					
8. Responds to conversation of peers, adults, or both (note in comment)					
9. Regularly initiates play with peers					
10. Initiates conversation with peers, adults or both (note in comment)					
11. Work/activity completion rate is age-appropriate					
12. Waits patiently as appropriate to age group					
13. Stays in assigned work location (stays in line, stays in circle)					
14. Speech and language is clear (words are recognized by most people)					
15. Takes visual cues from other students; follows the lead					
16. Sings or recites in unison with a group (poems, reading, or flag salute)					
17. Shares age appropriately (toys, games, snacks etc.)					
18. Asserts self *appropriately* when peer tries to take something or teases					
19. Does not exhibit stereotyped behavior (odd motor movements, visual focus, rigid routine)					
20. Plays with toys in a typical manner (drives a toy car; feeds doll; builds with blocks)					
21. Sustains attention to task for work					
22. Sustains focus on assigned (or chosen) play activity (specify assigned/chosen in comment)					
23. Imitates non-verbal physical actions (in song hand motions, exercises etc)					
24. Takes turns in activities with peers					
Total the number of **checks** (✓) in each column **Divide the Total by 24** to determine the percentage					
Percentage of Skills per Level					

Figure 2.1

School Participation Checklist: 4th – 8th Grade

Student: _____ Evaluator:_____Date: _____

Key: G = generalized; M = mastered; L = learning; N = not ready to learn; ✓ the demonstrated skill level

Activity/Skill/Behavior	G=0	M=1	L=2	N=3	Comment
1. Responds to classroom rules appropriately					
2. Uses appropriate touch to others (peers and adults)					
3. Stays focused on teacher when appropriate					
4. Responds to individual instructions					
5. Responds to group and conditional directions					
6. Typical class routines are followed without cues (locates seat, gets materials out)					
7. Does not isolate, hangs out with peers					
8. Responds to conversation of peers, adults, or both (note in comment)					
9. Regularly initiates social interaction with peers					
10. Initiates conversation with peers, adults or both (note in comment)					
11. Work/activity completion rate is age-appropriate					
12. Waits patiently as appropriate to age group					
13. Stays in assigned work location (stays in line, stays with group or team)					
14. Conversations and topics discussed are age-appropriate					
15. Takes visual cues from other students; follows the lead					
16. Sings or recites in unison with a group (flag salute, song)					
17. Shares age appropriately (balls, games, snacks etc.)					
18. Asserts self *appropriately* when peer tries to take something or is teased					
19. Does not exhibit stereotyped behavior (no rigid routines, odd or intense habits/interests)					
20. Uses age-appropriate objects/equipment in a typical manner (balls, Game Boy etc.)					
21. Sustains attention to task for work					
22. Sustains focus on assigned (or chosen) leisure activity (specify assigned/chosen in comment)					
23. Appropriately follows PE exercises and imitates other gross motor physical skills					
24. Takes turns in activities with peers (waits and recognizes when it is his/her turn)					
Total the number of **checks** (✓) in each column. Divide the Total by 24 to determine the percentage					
Percentage of Skills per Level					

Figure 2.2

School Participation Checklist: 9th – 12th Grade

Student: _____ Evaluator:_____Date: _____

Key: G = generalized; M = mastered; L = learning; N = not ready to learn; ✓ the demonstrated skill level

Activity/Skill/Behavior	G=0	M=1	L=2	N=3	Comment
1. Responds to classroom rules appropriately					
2. Maintains appropriate social distance from peers and adults					
3. Stays focused on teacher when appropriate					
4. Responds to individual instructions					
5. Responds to group and conditional directions					
6. Typical class routines are followed without cues (locates seat, gets materials out)					
7. Does not isolate, hangs out with peers					
8. Responds to conversation of peers, adults, or both (note in comment)					
9. Regularly initiates social interactions with peers					
10. Initiates conversation with peers, adults or both (note in comment)					
11. Work/activity completion rate is age-appropriate					
12. Waits patiently as appropriate to age group					
13. Stays in assigned work location (stays at desk, in line, with group or team)					
14. Conversation and topics are age-appropriate and varied					
15. Takes visual cues from other students; follows the lead in projects and activities					
16. Cheers, sings or recites in unison with a group (pep rallies, choir, flag salute,)					
17. Shares age appropriately objects, books, or food during social interaction					
18. Asserts self *appropriately* when peer teases or tries to manipulate a situation					
19. Does not exhibit stereotyped behavior (no rigid routines, odd or intense habits/interests)					
20. Uses age-appropriate objects/equipment in a typical manner (cell phone, iPod etc.)					
21. Sustains attention to task for work					
22. Sustains focus on assigned (or chosen) leisure activity (specify assigned/chosen in comment)					
23. Appropriately participates and follows exercises in PE, dances, or in other physical activities					
24. Takes turns in activities with peers (comment if in structured and/or unstructured situations)					
Total the number of **checks** (✓) in each column Divide the Total by 24 to determine the percentage					
Percentage of Skills per Level					

Figure 2.3

The SPC has also been used for student with disabilities other than ASD who are either already included in a general education setting, or who are being considered for a less restrictive setting. The SPC has been used with students who are considered "at risk" and the subject of a "Student Study Team". Very frequently students who are reviewed by a Student Study Team have been referred not just for academic needs, but also due to inappropriate student behaviors. The SPC has proven to be helpful in identifying areas of need for the student who considered at risk.

There is only one statement, number 19 on the checklist, which is more specific to students with ASD. This statement refers to stereotyped behavior which is somewhat disability specific. It is possible to redefine statement 19 on the SPC as perseverative behaviors or behaviors that interfere with learning when assessing students with other disabilities. A more complete description of stereotyped behaviors is found in Section 2 of this chapter.

What is the purpose of the SPC? The purpose of the checklist is always the same regardless of the student's disability. The SPC assists the IEP or SST team to determine the average student behaviors required in a specific inclusive setting and the student behavior skills demonstrated by the student who is being evaluated. If skill deficits can be identified prior to a student entering an inclusive setting and instruction provided to improve skills, there is a greater likelihood of successful participation in the inclusive classroom. If the student is already in the inclusive setting and differences are identified, then accommodations, modifications, instruction, and additional support may be implemented.

How can the data from the SPC be used? As one might predict a student with ASD or other disability often has difficulty fitting into an inclusive setting due to the student's lack of understanding of expected student behaviors. The staff may also not be aware of the instructional needs and supports that might be very helpful to support the student. The data gathered from the SPC is always used to support and possibly expand the opportunities and success for a student with ASD in the inclusive setting. Even when there is a large difference between the average student and the student with ASD the focus is on what needs to be added to the setting not exclusion from the inclusive setting. Thus, the data can be used for many purposes to build and support an inclusive setting such as:

- Build a shared perspective of student needs by a team.
- Clarification of basic student behaviors for a specific class.
- Identify present levels of functioning (strengths and needs).
- Baseline data for IEP goals.
- Skill areas for IEP goals.
- Pre-Post evaluation data.

What is the design of the SPC? The SPC is a simple checklist which identifies 24 typical student behaviors that are expected to be demonstrated at an age appropriate level by all students. This is not an all inclusive list, however the list does identify skills and student behaviors that educators value.

The list is organized in a random manner. This is intentional to prevent the educator completing the form from establishing a response pattern. When the checklist is scored the professional summarizing the information will separate the statements on the checklist into four categories. The categories are Patterns of Behavior, Attending, Communication, and Social Skills. There are six statements in each category.

The skills within each category are evaluated by the educator at four levels of acquisition. Skills are identified as Generalized, Mastered, Learning, or Not Ready. These levels of acquisition will be discussed in depth in Section 2 and 3. Each of these levels is assigned a point value which allows the evaluator to make a quantifiable comparison using three tables. These values assist the team in identifying skills for direct instruction. The scoring form also provides for the development of accommodations, modifications, and strategies that may be helpful in supporting the student with ASD or other disabilities in inclusive settings.

Is a formal signed assessment plan required when using the SPC? The answer to this question will vary according to local policies and procedures. To be in compliance it is recommended that the professional obtain district clarification prior to using the SPC. If there is a doubt, it is always best to proceed with official documentation which is a signed formal assessment plan.

Who requests the use of the SPC? Anyone who has knowledge of the SPC can request the use of it. Typically, it is the special education professional who is working with students in an inclusive setting that will make the request. Occasionally, a parent who is familiar with the SPC will request that it is used to prepare for transition to a new grade.

When is the request to use the SPC made? Typically the request is made during a formal meeting, when parents and professionals are discussing inclusive settings and the student's present levels. For the "at risk" student this may occur during a Student Study Team. During an eligibility assessment for special education, the evaluation team may seek informal information regarding the student's present levels of performance in basic student skills. Given this situation, a request to use the SPC may be made during an evaluation planning meeting. If the student is receiving services through an IEP then the request may be made during the IEP annual review or at other IEP or team meetings.

How often is the SPC used with a student? Usually the most frequently the SPC might be used is twice a year. When the SPC has been used with a student on a regular basis it is typically used at the beginning and/or end of the school year. It is used in the beginning of the school year to determine baseline information and identify skills to be taught or refined, as well as, identifying new accommodations, modification, and strategies that will be helpful at the new grade level. When the SPC is used at the end of the year it may be to prepare for transition and/or evaluate growth from the beginning of the year, if it had been used to determine baseline data.

It must be noted that the SPC may be used any time throughout the year when the student with disabilities is going to transition into a general education setting for full or part-time participation.

Who completes the SPC? The SPC was designed for completion by a general education teacher to establish the average student behavior for his or her classroom. The general education teacher would also complete the SPC on the student with disabilities if the general education teacher has had the student in class for at least two weeks.

Other staff members who have known the student with disabilities may also complete the SPC. These individuals would be selected based on the type of information the team is seeking to gather. More specific information on this question will be provided in Section 2.

How much time does it take to complete the SPC? It should not take a general educator more the 45 minutes to one hour to read the instructions and complete a checklist on an average student and the student with disabilities. Some special educators assist the general educator in completing the SPC on the student with disabilities by reading through the checklist with them. The special educator may clarify questions and probe for additional information for later reference. This practice may take a little longer; however it may save time later when the special educator is writing the report.

The answers to these frequently asked questions provide the foundation for understanding the School Participation Checklist. Questions regarding specific procedures and scoring will be answered in Section 2 and 3. This chapter is structured to give the reader a comprehensive method to evaluate "student behavior". The chapter also answer the question, "What do I do with the information I have gathered from the SPC?"

SECTION 2: PROCEDURES
Setting the Stage for the Successful Completion of the School Participation Checklist

The School Participation Checklist (SPC) is designed to collect information on expected student behaviors in a general education classroom. This information is to be collected on an average student and a student with ASD or other disabilities. In this chapter the student with ASD or another disability will be called the "focus student". Thus, the SPC is to always be completed by the general educator who either will be receiving a focus student or has the focus student in class on a regular basis.

The following list identifies reasons why other educators might complete the SPC, as well as the general educator.

- If the focus student spends part of his or her day in a Special Day Class (SDC), Resource room, or Learning Center the checklist can also be completed by the respective special educator. When scoring the SPC it is always interesting to compare the general and special education teacher's perspective.

- If there is an assistant that works with the focus student in the general education classroom, the assistant may also complete the checklist on the focus student.

- If the student is in a school program that requires him or her to see several different teachers each day, such as a middle or high school student, then one teacher is designated as the lead teacher. The lead teacher will fill out the SPC for the average student and the focus student. All the other teachers will fill out the SPC on the focus student only. Comparing the perspectives of all the teachers may help identify accommodations, modifications, and strategies that may be helpful in a class where the student might be struggling.

- Although it is not recommended, there may be times when is more appropriate to complete the checklist as a team. The need to do this might occur in a situation where there are many individuals working with a student in the same environment and a team perspective is required. When the form is completed as a team there must be consensus on each item. When consensus cannot be reached the team may come to an agreement by placing either a plus (+) or a minus (−) after the check in the box for the individual skill. The (+) and (–) are not scored numerically but may be noted in the report as clarification of skill level.

It is strongly recommended that each person complete the form independently. This gives the team the opportunity to evaluate different individual's perspectives of the student's ability to participate as a student in the various learning environments.

Occasionally, parents of the focus student have requested the opportunity to complete the SPC on their child. The reasons parents may make this request are varied. Typically they want to compare the behaviors that they see in community group settings or at home to the school environment. A few parents have wanted a comparison of each parent's perspective on the student behaviors of their child. The special educator who is scoring this SPC is encouraged to discuss the rationale thoroughly with the parents. As this is not a typical use of the SPC, and the decision to have the parents complete the checklist should be made only if the team feels that this information gathered would be a positive addition.

Author's Note: Although this situation happens infrequently, the parents have always been allowed to complete the SPC. Their responses have always been very insightful for both the parents and professionals.

The procedural steps for completing the SPC. The following outline details the steps that the special educator must take to assist the general educator or lead teacher, in the case of a middle or high school student, to successfully complete the SPC. Instructional procedures for the general educator are provided in a reproducible format on the CD in the back of this manual. The owner of this manual has permission to print the one page instruction sheet to assist the teacher completing the SPC.

1. **Provide the general educator with two copies of the SPC at the appropriate grade level.**

   - One checklist will be completed on an average student

   - The second will be completed on the focus student.

2. **To complete the SPC instruct the general educator to first select an average student from the class who is of the same gender and age as the focus student.**

   - This student should not be the best or the most challenging student in the class, but a representation of what is average for the class at the present time.

   - General educators have found it easier to identify an actual student who they consider as average, rather than try to create, in their mind, the skill level of a hypothetical average student. The student's name does not need to appear on the checklist. On the line provided for the name, the general educator may just write "Average" (boy or girl and the age or grade as appropriate). When considering the student behaviors of a preschool student it is important to always state the age of the student.

3. **Prior to completing the School Participation Checklist verify that the general educator understands the assessment terms.** It is very important that the general educator understands that a generalized skill is the highest and best skill level. Many times general educators think that the mastered level is the highest level. This misunderstanding can skew the results. Levels are defined as follows:

- **G** = Generalized: This is the best level of skill acquisition. The student owns the skill and uses it successfully in many environments with various people and with few to no reminders.

- **M** = Mastered: The student has mastered the skill about 80% of the time in one environment with specific people and prompts, but may have difficulty in other environments or with other people and needs more assistance or reminders to be successful.

- **L** = Learning: The student is actively engaged in learning this skill but has not reached a level of mastery in any environment and may require instruction or frequent prompting to demonstrate the skill.

- **NR** = Not Ready: The student is not aware of the skill or the need for the skill either cognitively or developmentally and requires constant reminders and support to demonstrate the skill.

4. **It is also very important that the term "stereotyped behavior" is defined clearly.** The words stereotyped behavior is part of the diagnostic criteria in the Diagnostic and Statistical Manual IV (1994) for Autistic Disorder. The behaviors include restricted and or repetitive interests or activities. These unusual patterns of behaviors are found, to some degree, in a student with ASD and are defined as follows:

- Interests that are narrow in focus, overly intense, and/ or unusual.
- Unreasonable insistence on sameness and following familiar routines.
- Repetitive motor mannerisms (hand flapping, finger flicking, toe walking).
- Preoccupation with parts of objects.

Dr. Sally Ozonoff, Dr. Geraldine Dawson and James McPartland (2002), provide many examples that will clarify the types of behaviors which might be seen when observing a student with ASD (See Figure 2.4). These descriptions may be helpful to a person who is explaining or completing the SPC. The reader is reminded that this is not an all inclusive list and that there is a range in level of intensity from very subtle to more intensive manifestation of stereotyped behaviors. It is also important to remember that any one individual with ASD may have some, but not all of these behaviors. A one page reproducible handout entitled a Closer Look at Stereotypical Behavior is provided on the CD at the back of this manual. This handout may be given to the general educator with the General Educator instruction sheet which is also on the CD.

5. Complete the SPC for the average student. Mark the box that best describes the skill level for the average student. Comments are not typically needed on the SPC for the average student.

6. After completing the checklist on the average student complete the second checklist form on the focus student. It is important to complete the checklist on the average student first because then the standard is established for the specific class.

Use the same criteria as listed above. Strongly encourage the educators to use the comment spaces to give details about their responses for clarification of the assessed level. The comments add to the understanding of the response and provide additional information if IEP goals are written on the skill. The comments also help the outside observer see a more complete picture of the student's behaviors that occur on a daily basis.

7. Provide the general educator with information on where to return the completed SPC. The information may be added to the general educator instruction sheet which is included on the CD in the back of this manual. The special educator is responsibility for scoring the SPC.

Interests that are narrow in focus, overly intense, and/or unusual:
- Very strong focus on particular topics to the exclusion of other topics
- Difficulty "letting go" of special topics or activities
  - Causing interference with other activities, thus causing delays eating or toileting due to focus on activity
- Interests in topics that are unusual for age
  - Sprinkler systems, movie ratings, astrophysics, radio station call letters, washers and/or dryers, road maps, medical terminology
- Excellent memory for details of special interest

Unreasonable insistence on sameness and following familiar routines
- Wants to perform certain activities in an exact order
  - Close car doors in specific order, videos stored by order of purchase date
- Easily upset by minor changes in routine
  - Taking a different route home from school
- Need for advanced warning of any changes
- Becomes highly anxious and upset if routines or rituals are not followed

Repetitive motor mannerisms
- Flapping hands when excited or upset
- Flicking fingers in front of eyes
- Odd hand postures or other hand movements
- Spinning or rocking for long periods of time
- Walking and/or running tiptoe

Preoccupation with parts of objects
- Uses objects in unusual ways, rather than the way of intended use
  - Flicks doll's eyes, repeatedly opens and closes doors on toy car, spins the wheel of the toy car, flicks puzzle pieces, lines up Legos® or sorts by color
- Interest in sensory qualities of objects
  - Sniffs objects, looks at objects closely, looks through objects, rubs or manipulate textures
- Likes objects that move
  - Fans, running water, spinning wheels
- Attachment to unusual object
  - Orange peel, string, shoe laces, strips of paper

Figure 2.4 Examples of Stereotype Behaviors

The checklist does not take long to complete, however at times teachers may need some assistance. If time permits the SPC may be completed as an interview. This allows for clarification of teacher responses and an opportunity to probe for additional information. It would also be appropriate to do a follow-up interview if the responses appear to be unusual or if there have been blank spaces left on the checklist. To successfully score the checklist all 24 statements must be marked.

Observations may also be made by other professionals. Observational notes may be added to the comments on the written report as a summary and a comparison to the SPC results.

SECTION 3: SCORING
THE SCHOOL PARTICIPATION CHECKLIST
Applying Quantifiable Values to Student Behavior

There are several steps to analyze the SPC. Each step is completed by using Tables 1- 6 in the scoring form. All the forms are provided in template and fill-in format for easy completion on the CD in the back of this manual. Each table presents a different aspect of the information derived from the completed checklist. These tables are simple, visual, and easy for both parents and professionals to understand. The tables in the scoring forms may be used in the presentation of the results, thus eliminating the need for a lengthy narrative report. Parents and professionals find this format very user friendly.

The steps and tables in the SPC scoring form include the following:

Step 1. Table 1: Analysis of Skill Categories

Step 2. Table 2: Percentage of Skills at Each Level of Achievement

Step 3. Table 3: Comparison of Average and Focus Students per Skill

Step 4. Table 4: Graphic Comparison of Total Scores for the Average and Focus Students.

Step 5. Table 5: Identification of Possible Skills for Instruction

Step 6. Table 6: Identification of Possible Accommodations, Modifications, and Strategies

Authors Note: Although there are three versions of the SPC to address student behaviors at various grade levels, only one scoring form is needed for Steps 2 - 6. Table 1 is customized for each grade level checklist. All the form templates and fill in formats are on the CD in the back of the manual.

Step 1. Analysis of Skill Categories. This first analysis will be completed using Table 1 (See Figure 2.5). Only the SPC that was filled out on the focus student is analyzed with Table 1. The average student's SPC will NOT be analyzed using Table 1 unless the scorer is using the fill-in forms on the CD which automatically scores both the average and focus student.

The purpose of this analysis is to give the team the skill level for each of the specific skills, now separated into the four categories that the SPC evaluates. The four skill categories the SPC evaluates are Patterns of Behavior, Attending, Communication, and Social Skills. The individual skills listed on the SPC are presented in a random order. By randomly listing the skills, the person completing the form is required to carefully evaluate each skill separately, not as a group of skills. Table 1 allows the scorer to reorganize

Patterns of Behavior	G=0	M=1	L=2	N=3
(1) Responds to classroom rules appropriately				✓
(2) Uses appropriate touch to others *(peers and adults)*		✓		
(6) Typical class routines are followed without cues				✓
(11) Work/activity completion rate is age-appropriate				✓
(12) Waits patiently as appropriate to age group			✓	
(19) Does not exhibit stereotyped behavior				✓
Attending				
(3) Stays focused on teacher when appropriate				✓
(5) Responds to group and conditional directions				✓
(13) Stays in assigned work location (e.g. stays in line, stays in circle)			✓	
(15) Takes visual cues from other students; follows the lead				✓
(21) Sustains attention to task for work			✓	
(22) Sustains focus on assigned (or chosen) play activity			✓	
Communication/Language:				
(4) Responds to individual instructions				✓
(8) Responds to conversation of peers, adults, or both			✓	
(10) Initiates conversation with peers, adults, or both			✓	
(14) Speech is clear (words are recognized by most people)	✓			
(16) Sings or recites in unison with group				✓
(23) Imitates non-verbal physical actions (in song hand motions, exercises)				✓
Social Skills				
(7) Does not isolate, stays near or with peers				✓
(9) Regularly initiates play with peers			✓	
(17) Shares age-appropriately (e.g. toys, games, snacks etc.)				✓
(18) Appropriately asserts self when a peer tries to take something or teases	✓			
(20) Plays with toys in a typical manner (drives toy car, feeds doll etc)			✓	
(24) Takes turn in activities with peers				✓

Figure 2.5 Table 1 Analysis of Skill Categories (Preschool - 3rd Grade SAMPLE)

all the skills in each category and review skill level per category. This format gives the team a more complete visual picture of the student's levels, rather than the numerical presentation used in the other scoring tables. The three versions of Table 1 align with the grade level SPC forms which are found on the CD at the end of the manual.

This analysis is completed by looking for the numbered skills in each category on the completed SPC for the focus student. Mark the level of achievement indicated on the SPC by checking the same box (G, M, L, or N) on Table 1. A completed sample is shown in Figure 2.5.

Step 2. Calculate the Percentage of Skills at Each Level of Achievement. These scores are taken from the last row of the completed SPC (See figure 2.6).

The person scoring the SPC counts the number of skills checked in each column. This number becomes the numerator over a denominator of 24, which is the number of skills possible per column. The denominator is then divided into the numerator to arrive at the percentage of skills in each category. Figure 2.7 provides a percentage chart to assist in the manual completion of Table 2. This procedure is done on the completed SPC for both the average student and the focus student. Table 2 provides the team with the first numerical comparison of average student skills/ behaviors to the skill level of the focus student.

School Participation Checklist: Preschool – 3rd Grade

Student: _Focus Kindergarten Student_ Evaluator:_____Date:_____

Key: G = generalized; M = mastered; L = learning; N = not ready to learn; ✓ the demonstrated skill level

Activity/Skill/Behavior	G=0	M=1	L=2	N=3	Comment
1. Responds to classroom rules appropriately				✓	No understanding of rules yet
2. Uses appropriate touch to others (peers and adults)		✓			Likes to keep his hands to himself
3. Stays focused on teacher when appropriate				✓	Very rarely
4. Responds to individual instructions				✓	Only when one has his full attention
5. Responds to group and conditional directions				✓	Always is doing his own thing
6. Typical class routines are followed without cues (puts backpack away, gets in line)				✓	Doesn't pay much attention to peers
7. Does not isolate, stays near or with peers				✓	Near peers, not aware of the peers
8. Responds to conversation of peers, adults, or both (note in comment)			✓		
9. Regularly initiates play with peers			✓		
10. Initiates conversation with peers, adults or both (note in comment)			✓		
11. Work/activity completion rate is age-appropriate				✓	Cannot stay with task without 1:1 adult support
12. Waits patiently as appropriate to age group			✓		
13. Stays in assigned work location (stays in line, stays in circle)			✓		
14. Speech and language is clear (words are recognized by most people)	✓				Talks like a little adult, but always on his own topic
15. Takes visual cues from other students; follows the lead				✓	Doesn't pay much attention to peers
16. Sings or recites in unison with a group (poems, reading, or flag salute)				✓	Stays with group, no participate
17. Shares age appropriately (toys, games, snacks etc.)				✓	Likes to keep all his trains to himself
18. Asserts self *appropriately* when peer tries to take something or teases	✓				Says "NO" and finds a staff
19. Does not exhibit stereotyped behavior (odd motor movements, visual focus, rigid routine)				✓	Walks on his toes; hand flaps; always talks about trains
20. Plays with toys in a typical manner (drives a toy car; feeds doll; builds with blocks)			✓		
21. Sustains attention to task for work			✓		
22. Sustains focus on assigned (or chosen) play activity (specify assigned/chosen in comment)			✓		
23. Imitates non-verbal physical actions (in song hand motions, exercises etc)				✓	Does not do hand motions in songs; occasionally imitates exercises
24. Takes turns in activities with peers				✓	Will do this but, only with prompting
Total the number of checks (✓) in each column Divide the Total by 24 to determine the percentage	2/24	1/24	8/24	13/24	
Percentage of Skills per Level	8%	4%	33%	54%	

Figure 2.6 Completed School Participation checklist

# of Skills	%	# of Skills	%	# of Skills	%
1	4%	9*	38%	17*	71%
2	8%	10*	42%	18	75%
3*	13%	11*	46%	19	79%
4*	17%	12	50%	20	83%
5	21%	13	54%	21*	88%
6	25%	14	58%	22*	92%
7	29%	15*	63%	23*	96%
8	33%	16*	67%	24	100%

Figure 2.7 Percentage Chart for Skill at Each Level of Achievement

The (*) indicates that the percentage was not even. These percentages were rounded up to the next highest number. The scorer may need to adjust these percentages down by .5 so the four levels of achievement equal a total of 100%. The rounding up or down should be done on an individual basis.

When the calculations have been completed the percentages for both the average and focus students are transferred to Table 2 (See Figure 2.8). This table provides the first numerical comparison.

Table 2: Percentage of Scores at each Level of Achievement

	Generalized	Mastered	Learning	Not ready
Average Student	67%	29%	4%	0%
Focus Student	8%	4%	33%	54%

Figure 2.8

Step 3. Comparison of Average and Focus Students per Skill. Table 3 is used to reports this information. (See Figure 2.10) The numerical values for each skill level can be found in the top row of the SPC. The values were assigned to indicate the amount of support or instruction a student requires on each skill at the present time. The numerical range is 0 to 3. The best score a student can earn is a (0) which means that the skill is generalized and requires little to no support. An evaluation tool where the lower skill is best can be confusing to some, thus this difference may need additional explanation. See Figure 2.9 for the rubric supporting the scoring system.

G = 0	**Generalization:** The student requires little to no intervention/support with this skill. The skill is demonstrated across many settings, with different people. This is the best score which means the lowest score equals highest skill level.
M = 1	**Mastered:** The student requires only occasional intervention about 80% of the time. The skill is used efficiently in one setting with a specific individual, the student requires more prompts to do the skill in other settings with other individuals.
L = 2	**Learning:** The student requires frequent interventions and direct instruction. The student is beginning to demonstrate acquisition of the skill with direct instruction. The student is engaged in the learning process.
N = 3	**Not Ready:** The student requires constant intervention and support from staff. At this time the student lacks any awareness of this skill and his/her need to use the skill in the classroom or on the school campus. May require staff in close proximity.

Figure 2.9 Scoring Rubric

Table 3 is completed from information gathered on the SPC for both the average and the focus student. The 0 to 3 numerical scoring system is used to score both students (See Figure 2.9). When transferring the information to Table 3, for the focus student the scorer may review Table 1, which presents the skills in their respective categories; however, now the scorer will assign a point value to the skill. To score the average student the scorer will need to review the SPC and reorganize the skills by category and assign the point value in the respective box for each skill on Table 3, unless the scorer is using the fill-in forms on the CD. There are three columns per category. The first column is the number of the skill as it appears on the SPC. The second column is for the scores of the average student. The third column is for the scores of the focus student. When all the scores have been entered in the columns, the numbers in each column should be totaled and recorded in the bottom row. Figure 2.10 provides a look at Table 3 when it is completed for both students.

Table 3: Comparison of Average and Focus Students per Skill across Categories

Patterns of Behavior			Attending			Communication			Social Skills		
	Avg.	Focus		Avg.	Focus		Avg.	Focus		Avg.	Focus
1.	0	3	3.	0	3	4.	0	3	7.	0	3
2.	0	1	5.	0	3	8.	0	2	9.	0	2
6.	1	3	13.	0	2	10.	0	2	17.	0	3
11.	0	3	15.	2	3	14.	0	0	18.	1	0
12.	0	2	21.	1	2	16.	1	3	20.	0	2
19.	0	3	22.	1	2	23.	1	3	24.	1	3
total	1	15	total	4	15	total	2	13	total	2	13

Figure 2.10

Step 4. Graphic Comparison of Total Scores per Student. Table 4 is designed to take the total scores from Table 3 and present them graphically in terms of potential percent of instruction and support needed to perform successfully in a general education setting (See Figure 2.11).

Table 4: Graphic Comparison of Total Scores

Total Score	% of Instruction/ Support Needed	Patterns of Behavior	Attending	Communication	Social Skills
18	100%				
17	90%				
16					
15	80%	Focus Student	Focus Student		
14					
13	70%			Focus Student	Focus Student
12					
11	60%				
10					
9	50%				
8	40%				
7					
6	30%				
5					
4	20%		Average Student		
3					
2	10%			Average Student	Average Student
1		Average Student			
0					

Figure 2.11 Shaded area indicates typical range of scores for the average student

Table 4 is divided into six columns. The first column lists the total possible scores per each column on Table 3. The scores in this column range from 0 to 18. The highest score a student can receive is 18, which means that the student scored a 3 in each of the 6 skill areas (3 X 6=18). A student that receives a score of 18 needs support in the inclusive setting 100% of the time, as the higher the score the greater the need for support. In converse the student who scores six or less has more skills and appropriate student behaviors. The area between six and zero is shaded and represents the range in which most general educators rate their average students. The average student only scores outside this range when it is developmentally appropriate, as with preschool students; or when the specific class of students, as a whole, has difficulty with student behavior. More longitudinal data is presented in Appendix A.

The second column represents an approximate percentage of the amount of instruction and/or support the focus student and average student might need to be successful in an inclusive setting. The percentages were determined by dividing every possible student score by 18, which are the most points possible. For example, a score of 9 divided by 18 equals 50%. Only the even percentages were listed on Table 4. The shading in the rows is added for visual separation of the percentage groups. The blank rows represent the range between the percentages.

The next four columns represent each skill category. The total score from each category on Table 3 is located in column one on Table 4. The scorer finds the student's score in column one on Table 4, then follows the row to the respective category and enters either the student's initials or "Focus Student" or "Average Student" as shown in Figure 2.11.

The visual representation presented in Tables 2, 3, and 4 (See Figures 2.8, 2.10, and 2.11) have proven very helpful in developing a plan to support the student who demonstrates many academic skills, but as one mother said is, "Socially clueless". By incorporating the SPC into an assessment plan a team may report a quantifiable difference in student behavior which oftentimes results in unconventional behaviors that result in frustration for both the student and the staff. This is a concrete example of how a student who may be able to cite rules and pass standardized tests in social pragmatics, in the general education setting has challenges performing basic student behaviors, often does not have a friend, and is usually literally and figuratively on the outside looking in.

Step 5. Identification of Possible Skills for Instruction. Table 5 addresses the areas that might be considered for direct instruction in IEP goals. Typically skills with a score of 2, learning, would be placed on Table 5 (See Figure 2.12). Skills that were considered mastered, or scored a 1, may be considered for instruction across environments, other people and with varied instructions to move the focus student to the generalized level. Skills that are scored in the 'not ready' range might be included if the focus student is beginning to demonstrate signs that the skill is emerging. Often times the "not ready" skills may be addressed as part of the school routine. The team must discuss and prioritize which skills should be addressed and at what level of intensity.

Table 5: Identification of Possible Skills for Instruction

Patterns of Behavior: (2)　Uses appropriate touch to others, primarily peers   (12) Waits patiently as appropriate to age group
Attending: (13) Stays in assigned work location (stays in line, stays in circle)   (21) Sustains attention to task for work   (22) Sustains focus on assigned play activity
Communication: (8)　Responds to conversation of peers   (10) Initiates conversation with peers
Social Skills: (9)　Regularly initiates play with peers   (20) Plays with toys in a typical manner

Figure 2.12

Step 6. Identification of Possible Accommodations, Modifications, and Strategies. Table 6 offers suggestions to assist in the implementation of goals and possible accommodation and modifications that might be helpful (See Figure 2.13). Section 4 and 5 in this chapter discuss the possible options for Table 5.

Summary Comments. The final section of the scoring form includes an area in which a short report might be written. This is an option for the scorer of the SPC. Often the scorer has also completed an observation which will provide additional information or responses to questions the team posed when the request for the SPC was made (See Figure 2.15). The statement in Figure 2.14 is always included to explain the form and function of the SPC.

Table 6: Possible Accommodations, Modifications, and Strategies

Patterns of Behavior: 1. Make classroom rules visual with opportunities to review the rules as part of the daily routine. 2. Consider the use of Social Stories™ to concretely explain the purpose and perspective of rules. 3. Systematically and visually reinforce all appropriate behavior. 4. Use a visual schedule and a visual to do list that individually explains expectations. 5. Consider the use of a visual timer. 6. Teach wait across activities with the use of a visual wait card. 7. Identify stereotyped behaviors that impede learning and decide on replacement behaviors.
Attending: 1. Systematically reinforce looking at the teacher, staying in place and on task for work time and finishing assigned task. 2. Consider using a visual cue as a focus point to train keeping his eyes on the teacher. 3. Organize task visually to have a clear beginning and end. 4. Structure imitation activities to attend to the actions of peers. This can be done in a game format. 5. Redirect him to notice what a reliable peer is doing and say "Do that."
Communication: 1. Play games that require following individual instructions. 2. Systematically reinforce spontaneously following instructions. 3. Consider the use of drama and comic strip conversations to establish reciprocal conversation practice with peers. 4. Reinforce participation in songs and musical activities; consider the use of priming.
Social Skills: 1. Facilitate positive peer interactions with various students. 2. Teach games and related skills in a structured manner with adult and/or peer coaching. 3. Keep the student actively involved in reciprocal peer interactions with adult support. 4. Role play alternate responses to situations where the student makes social mistakes. 5. Systematically reinforce, with a visual system, appropriate social interactions.

Figure 2.13

Comments to the IEP/SST team: This checklist is a non-standardized tool. It is designed simply to give a snapshot of an average peer of the same age and gender to the student who is being assessed. The list is comprised of basic school participation skills that are needed for successful participation in a school environment. This is not an all inclusive list and should only be considered as a small part of a more complete assessment and extensive observation.

Figure 2.14

Additional Comments:

The focus student was observed in his classroom and on the playground at recess. Strengths observed include good cognitive skills and good speech when he chooses to use it. Areas of concern include his inflexibility, poor transitions, loud verbal protests that are sustained for extended periods of time, need for sameness and exact compliance to nonfunctional routines.

Characteristics of an Autism Spectrum Disorder include marked impairments in reciprocal social interaction, communication, and restricted patterns of behavior. The focus student presented behaviors that could be classified under each of these categories, such as lack of awareness of peers, impaired nonverbal communication and lack of development of friends. He does interact better with adults; however this too is on his own terms. His vocal quality, prosody, is somewhat unusual; however he used good syntax and grammar when he was speaking on topics of interest. His vocal quality was tense and less mature when he was in an academic situation. He lacked social and communicative reciprocity in most situations. He did initiate a request to use markers instead of crayons and accepted a "no" when told the markers were not for the project. He has definite areas of interest that are unusual and intense in nature, such as his large paper coins.

Figure 2.15 Sample report to summarize Additional Information

SECTION 4: STRATEGIES

Great Practices and Resources to Consider

The following lists of suggested strategies are organized across the four categories of student skills as grouped on the School Participation Checklist. The strategies are not presented by age groups; however all the strategies are applicable to any age group given the appropriate changes. These suggested ideas are based on recognized best practices for working with students with ASD. Pivotal strategies and methods for instruction have been developed by the following authors and programs: Treatment and Education of Autistic and Related Communication Handicapped Children (TEACCH) (2003), Picture Exchange Communication System (PECS) (2002), Applied Behavior Analysis (ABA), social thinking activities from Carol Gray, (1993,1994,2004) Michelle Garcia Winner, (2002) Jeanette McAfee (2002), and Amelia Davies (2004). This is not an all inclusive list and should be added to other strategies that have proven to work well.

When considering the many strategies for working with children with ASD, two key thoughts should be kept in mind; keep things simple and make instruction visual. While maintaining those thoughts one must also consider the learning environment, the structure of the classroom and the powerful resource that peers may provide to teachers in support of the focus student. As research shows, motivated peers can make a difference in the lives of students with disabilities, but when the peers are given instruction and support in teaching their classmates with disabilities, much greater growth will be achieved. (Ozonoff, Rogers, and Hendren 2003) Chapter 6 provides activities for developing friendship between the average student and a student with ASD.

Patterns of Behavior: Skills 1, 2, 6, 11, 12, 19

- Make classroom rules visual with pictures or icons to represent the rules.
  - Provide opportunities to review the rules as part of the daily routine.
  - Role play rules periodically when rules are being obeyed.
  - Systematically and visually reinforce following the rules.
  - Consider the use of Social Stories^{TM} (Gray, 1993 & 2004) to concretely explain the purpose and perspective of rules.
  - Consider the use of Comic Strip Conversation (Gray, 1994) to concretely explain how a rule was broken and how to handle it differently in the future.
  - Consider the use of White Board Words and Thoughts (Lighthall and Schetter 2008) to make transient words 3 dimensional and understand the thoughts of others when rules are broken.
- Consider the use of behavioral mapping (Winner, 2002) to explain using appropriate touch with peers.
- Consider the use of a graphic organizer or a "Thinking Tool" to understand the relationship of actions to outcomes (Schetter, 2004).

- Identify the function behind an inappropriate student behavior, such as touching others and identify and teach a replacement behavior. (See Section 6: Case Study).

- Systematically and visually reinforce all appropriate behavior.

- Use a visual schedule and/or a visual to do list that individually explains expectations.

  - Reinforce positive use of the form or system.

- Consider the use of a visual timer.

- Chunk work into smaller segments.

- Establish a visual system to reinforce a quick finish; the reinforcement must be highly motivational and could be determined by the student prior to beginning his work.

- Teach the concept of waiting or "wait" across activities with the use of a visual wait card (Frost & Bondy, 2004).

- Develop a wait box filled with a few items that a student could use while waiting.

- Shape waiting behavior by requiring a short wait at first, the gradually increase the wait time.

  - Always systematically reinforce appropriate waiting.

- Identify stereotyped behaviors that impede learning and determine the function of the behaviors.

  - Decide if replacement behaviors are required.

  - Certain stereotyped behaviors may be structured and used as reinforcers.

Attending: Skills 3, 5, 13, 15, 21, 22

- Consider using a visual cue as a focus point, to train the student to keep his eyes on the teacher; the cue could be a picture or symbol:

  - Start teaching this in a game format or in small group.

  - Systematically reinforce looking at or towards the teacher.

- Structure imitation activities that teach attending to the actions of peers. This can be done in a game format.

- Determine how long a student is able to stay in his assigned place.

  - Have the student stay in the assigned place for 50-75% of the amount of time he usually can sit; reinforce his success.

- Systematically reinforce a student's ability to stay in an assigned place across all environments.

- Redirect him to notice what a reliable peer is doing and say "Do that".

- Structure activities or games that require imitating peers, such as exercises or pretending to be a mirror to a peer; simplify the games as required for the age group.

- Ask student to describe what peers are doing; this can be naturally occurring actions or in a game format.

- Consider the use of a visual timer to clearly identify how much time must be spent in each activity.

- Use a visual work system to break activity into manageable portions to encourage the ability to stay on task with an activity for longer periods of time (Mesibov et. al 2003 and 2004)

Communication: Skills 4, 8, 10, 14, 16, 23

- Play games that require following individual instructions, such as Red Light-Green Light or Simon Says.
- List instructions visually on the board or on a personal list; the personal list may be a "to do" list format.
- Provide a list with check off boxes that visual identify the concept of "all done" as the student marks each box.
- Systematically reinforce spontaneously following instructions across the day and environments.
- Consider the use of drama (Davies, 2004) and comic strip conversations (Gray, 1994) and White Board Words and Thoughts (Lighthall and Schetter 2008) to establish reciprocal conversation practice with peers.
- Train peers to facilitate a conversation.
- Use visual conversation games that make reciprocal exchanges visual, such as the "Conversation Tree" by Michelle Garcia-Winner (2002).
- Additional strategies for conversation skills are discussed in *Navigating the Social World* by Jeanette McAfee (2002).
- When clarity of speech is an issue enlist the assistance of a speech therapist.
- Consider the use of "priming" (Wilde, Koegel & Koegel, 1992) by informally introducing new materials or concepts that will be covered in class in the future, either at home or at

an informal time at school, prior to formal instruction in the classroom.

- Practice reading or reciting aloud in small groups and gradually increase the size of the group.

- Practice nonverbal imitation activities as a foundation to hand motions in songs.

- Teach hand motions to songs with the priming method (Wilde, Koegel & Koegel, 1992) and in very small groups with limited distraction. Combining singing and motor movements requires multi-tasking, which often is a significant challenge to many students with ASD.

Social Skills: Skills 7, 9, 17, 18, 20, 24

- Desensitize children who isolate by introducing only one peer at a low stress time; as tolerance increases either add another peer or increase the length of time the child spends with one peer.

- Facilitate positive peer interactions with various students by providing adult support and planning.

- Teach games and related skills in a structured manner with adult and/or peer coaching at typical play times like recess. See Section 6 for a case study.

- Use "communication temptations" to set up opportunities to initiate social interaction with peers and other adults.

- Comic Strip Conversations by Carol Gray (1994) are a strategy to make initiation and turn taking skills visual and provide a basis for teaching perspective taking and social understanding of reciprocal play and social conversations in play.

- White Board Words and Thoughts (Lighthall and Schetter 2008) provide hands on activities with white boards in specific shapes to allow the student the opportunity to manipulate the conversation with the shape of the white board representing thoughts, feelings, comments, and requests or questions.

- Play games that require initiation and/or turn taking with peers who understand the skill the focus student is currently learning.

- Reinforce all initiation and/or turn taking when it is a deficit area.

- Provide structured opportunities to share neutral items with adult or peer facilitation (this is also a procedure to teach turn taking).
  - Gradually increase the structured sharing to those items that are more highly preferred; begin with turn taking for a short duration of time and increase the time as the student develops a level of trust and comfort.

- Provide opportunities to practice and generalize sharing during less structure times, after the student is able to share in a structured setting.

- Systematically reinforce sharing in a visual way using differential strategies (better reward for the spontaneous intentional sharing).

- Systematically teach appropriate refusal to share or actions to retrieve an item that has been taken.
  - Making this instruction visual is very important; the following strategies are helpful in teaching this skill:

- Basic Critical Thinking forms, Patricia Schetter (2004).
- Behavioral Mapping, Michelle Garcia-Winner (2002).
- Comic Strip Conversations, Carol Gray (1994).
- Coping with stressors may also need to be addressed when developing appropriate responses to classroom and playground situations.
  - Using a visual such as a barometer or thermometer as suggested by Jeanette McAfee (2002), or a 5 point scale (Buron 2003) may be helpful.
- Role play alternate responses to situations where social mistakes are made; A game called "Cool – Not Cool" gives children a chance to role play either correct or incorrect responses to a social situation and have the group give a thumbs up or down as an indication of their interpretation of what they just saw.
  - The students may video tape this activity or play it in a game show format.
- Teach appropriate play with toys by structuring play sequences or scripts.
  - Many strategies for play are outlined by Pamela Wolfberg (2003).
- Systematically reinforce, with a visual system, all appropriate social interactions that are identified for direct instruction.
- Establish baseline data and develop a plan for recording data to show progress. The case study presented in Section 6 provides and example of data on teaching recess skills.

SECTION 5: ACCOMMODATIONS AND MODIFICATIONS
A Form to Support the Accommodations and Modifications
for the School Participation Checklist

Prior to using accommodations and modifications the terms must first be clearly defined. The following are the generally accepted educational definitions.

Accommodations are changes made within the classroom which provide access for a student with a disability to participate in the general education curriculum which do not fundamentally alter or lower the standard or expectation of content mastery. Basic accommodations include changes in quantity, time, input, output, participation and level of support. Each of these areas should be individualized for each student.

Modifications are changes in the classroom instruction or expectations, which may appear to be similar to accommodations but which do fundamentally alter or lower the standard or expectations of the instructional objectives of the activities. Basic modifications may include level of difficulty, alternate goals, or a substitute curriculum. These modifications will be individualized based on assessed needs as outlines in the student's IEP.

When determining the appropriateness of accommodations and modifications for a student the IEP team must base their decision on present levels, special factors, IEP goals, services, and setting for the implementation of goals. If the IEP team has determined that the general education classroom is the appropriate setting in which to implement the student's goals then it is critical to for the IEP team to identify the accommodations and modifications that will be implemented in the general education setting and documented them on the IEP. The expectation for an included student is that they will participate like the average student, unless there is an accommodation and modification that allows for a different level of participation documented on the IEP.

Typically the IEP team identifies accommodations and/or modifications which address the curriculum and academic skills. However, besides just accessing the general curriculum and gaining academic skills there is typically also a goal to increase social and appropriate student behavior. If the SPC has been used to assist the team in identifying student behavior skills, the scorer of the SPC will identify accommodations and modifications to be considered by the IEP team. These suggestions are listed on Table 6 of the Scoring Form (See Figure 2.13).

The following Figures 2.16, 2.17, 2.18, and 2.19 provide some ideas of accommodations and modification which align with the School Participation Checklist. The suggestions for accommodation are presented under the standard types of changes including quantity, time, input, output, participation and level of support. Modifications are listed in the same manner including reducing the level of difficulty, alternate goals, or a substitute curriculum. Suggestions are presented for each skill category of the SPC. This is not an all inclusive list and is provided to give implementers some ideas as a starting point when developing an individualized plan for accommodations and modifications.

These accommodations and modifications have been incorporated into a checklist that may be used with the SPC or as a stand alone form when a team is addressing issues of student behavior verses just academic considerations. A reproducible copy of "SPC Accommodation and Modification Planning Form" is available in the CD in the back of this manual and is shown in Figure 2.a

Patterns of Behavior: Skills # 1, 2, 6, 11, 12, 19	
Accommodations	**Modifications**
Quantity: reduce number of rules **Time:** allow more time on task or don't require a long wait time **Input:** present information visually **Input:** teach wait using a visual wait card **Output:** provide a visual checklist, to do list, or a work system to follow routines **Level of Support:** assign extra help either by a peer or adult **Level of Support:** use a visual timer to assist in prompt work completion	**Difficulty:** simplify rules **Difficulty:** only required to complete a 1 – 2 step routine **Alternate Goal:** require alternate task that is less complex if activity is over stimulating **Substitute Curriculum:** follows different participation rules **Substitute Curriculum:** time is scheduled for participation in sensory diet activities while class is doing math and written assignments

Figure 2.16 Sample Accommodations and Modifications for Patterns of Behavior

| Attending: Skills # 3, 5, 13, 15, 21, 22 ||
Accommodations	Modifications
Quantity: is not required to stay at his desk for more than 15 minutes **Time:** looks at teacher for short periods of time **Input:** give visual cue with timers, color coding, point of reference near teacher to keep his eyes forward **Output:** reinforcement is given for longer periods of time with non-preferred activities **Level of Support:** trained peers direct attention with gestural prompts	**Difficulty:** only present work at student's level not general class level **Difficulty:** will follow personal schedule **Alternate Goal:** participation in games require student to follow only part of the activity (running with a group that stops so he can kick the soccer ball) **Substitute Curriculum:** focus on life skills with the length of attending requirements completely different from the class in all academic areas

Figure 2.17 Sample Accommodations and Modifications for Attending

| Communication: Skills # 4, 8, 10, 14, 16, 23 ||
Accommodations	Modifications
Quantity: reinforce 2 or more initiations or responses to conversations **Time:** schedule a specific time for conversations **Input:** put verbal instructions in written format **Input:** set up communication temptations **Output:** accept one word or short phrase response **Output:** require either verbal or physical response but not both **Level of Support:** train peers how to communicate with student	**Difficulty:** keep language simple; give only 1 instruction at a time **Difficulty:** initiates request by handing a picture to a peer or adult **Alternate Goals:** for oral reports the student will set the timer and ring the bell when the allotted is up (working on his goal of time and attending) **Substitute Curriculum:** use an augmented system with pictures, assistive devices or sign language to communicate

Figure 2.18 Sample Accommodations and Modifications for Communication

Social Skills: Skills # 7, 9 ,17, 18, 20, 24	
Accommodations	**Modifications**
Quantity: limit number of members in a work group to 1-2 other students **Quantity:** limit or increase the number of social activities and interactions or toys that are available at one time **Time:** use a visual cue (card or gesture) to allow the student to limit his time in a group activity **Time:** shorten or lengthen the amount of time spent on social interaction or play with toys **Input:** select certain children to interact with student **Input:** set out only the toys required for an activity **Input:** use video to teach play skills **Output:** when learning a new activity allow the student to choose to discontinue after the activity has been completed once **Level of Support:** provide expert peers or adult support to learn and generalize new social activities	**Difficulty:** simplify or change the rules of games **Difficulty:** reduce the environmental demands (lower the basketball hoop) **Alternate Goal:** group is working on soccer skills and the focus student is working on increasing ability to sustain a running pace. **Alternate Goal:** group is playing a game and focus student is learning to take turns **Substitute Curriculum:** students are working in cooperative learning groups for science, focus student is learning to stay with a group and label objects

Figure 2.19 Sample Accommodations and Modifications for Social Skills

R. - Readiness of Student Behavior

School Participation Checklist
Accommodation and Modification Planning Form

Student: _____ Grade/Class(es): _____ Date: _____

Team developing the plan: _____

Persons responsible for implementation: _____

This form is to assist a team in planning supports for inclusive settings. Check the Accommodation of Modification that might be helpful in the left column. This is only a list of ideas. Teams are encouraged to add other ideas. Describe the specific consideration for the focus student.

Possible Accommodations	Specifics for Individualized Student Plan
Patterns of Behavior: Skills # 1, 2, 6, 11, 12, 19	
☐ Quantity: reduce number of rules ☐ Time: allow more time on task or don't require a long wait time ☐ Input: present information visually ☐ Input: teach wait using a visual wait card ☐ Output: provide a visual checklist, to do list, or a work system to follow routines ☐ Level of Support: assign extra help either by a peer or adult ☐ Level of Support: use a visual timer to assist in prompt work completion ☐ Other:	
Attending: Skills # 3, 5, 13, 15, 21, 22	
☐ Quantity: is not required to stay at his desk for more than 15 minutes ☐ Time: looks at teacher for short periods of time ☐ Input: give visual cue with timers, color coding, point of reference near teacher to keep his eyes forward ☐ Output: reinforcement is given for longer periods of time with non-preferred activities ☐ Level of Support: trained peers direct attention with gestural prompts ☐ Other:	
Communication: Skills # 4, 8, 10, 14, 16, 23	
☐ Quantity: reinforce 2 or more initiations or responses to conversations ☐ Time: schedule a specific time for conversations ☐ Input: put verbal instructions in written format ☐ Input: set up communication temptations ☐ Output: accept one word or short phrase response ☐ Output: require either verbal or physical response but not both ☐ Level of Support: train peers how to communicate with student ☐ Other:	

Figure 2.a School Participation Checklist page 1

71

R.E.A.D.Y. for Inclusion

Possible Accommodations	Specifics for Individualized Student Plan
Social Skills: Skills # 7, 9 ,17, 18, 20, 24	
☐ **Quantity:** limit or increase the number of social activities and interactions or toys that are available at one time ☐ **Time:** use a visual cue (card or gesture) to allow the student to limit his time in a group activity ☐ **Time:** shorten or lengthen the amount of time spent on social interaction or play with toys ☐ **Input:** select certain children to interact with student ☐ **Input:** set out only the toys required for an activity ☐ **Input:** use video to teach play skills ☐ **Output:** when learning a new activity allow the student to choose to discontinue after the activity has been completed once ☐ **Level of Support:** provide expert peers or adult support to learn and generalize new social activities ☐ **Other:**	

Possible Modification	Specifics for Individualized Student Plan
Patterns of Behavior: Skills # 1, 2, 6, 11, 12, 19	
☐ **Difficulty:** simplify rules ☐ **Difficulty:** only required to complete a 1 – 2 step routine ☐ **Alternate Goal:** require alternate task that is less complex if activity is over stimulating ☐ **Substitute Curriculum:** follows different participation rules ☐ **Substitute Curriculum:** time is scheduled for participation in sensory diet activities while class is doing math and written assignments ☐ **Other:**	
Attending: Skills # 3, 5, 13, 15, 21, 22	
Alternate Goals: ☐ **Difficulty:** only present work at student's level not general class level ☐ **Difficulty:** will follow personal schedule ☐ **Alternate Goal:** participation in games require student to follow only part of the activity (running with a group that stops so he can kick the soccer ball) ☐ **Substitute Curriculum:** focus on life skills with the length of attending requirements completely different from the class in all academic areas ☐ **Other:**	

Figure 2.a School Participation Checklist page 2

72

Possible Modification	Specifics for Individualized Student Plan
Communication: Skills # 4, 8, 10, 14, 16, 23	
☐ **Difficulty:** keep language simple; give only 1 instruction at a time ☐ **Difficulty:** initiates request by handing a picture to a peer or adult ☐ **Alternate Goals:** for oral reports the student will set the timer and ring the bell when the allotted is up (working on his goal of time and attending) ☐ **Substitute Curriculum:** use an augmented system with pictures, assistive devices or sign language to communicate ☐ **Other:**	
Social Skills: Skills # 7, 9 ,17, 18, 20, 24	
☐ **Difficulty:** simplify or change the rules of games ☐ **Difficulty:** reduce the environmental demands (lower the basketball hoop) ☐ **Alternate Goal:** group is working on soccer skills and the focus student is working on increasing ability to sustain a running pace ☐ **Alternate Goal:** group is playing a game and focus student is learning to take turns ☐ **Substitute Curriculum:** students are working in cooperative learning groups for science, focus student is learning to stay with a group and label objects ☐ **Other:**	

Figure 2.a School Participation Checklist page 3

SECTION 6: DEVELOPING MEASURABLE ANNUAL GOALS
A Case Study Reveals How to Teach Recess

The previous Sections have provided tools to identify areas of student behavior that may require specific instruction to reach mastery and generalization. Suggestions and a checklist have also been provided for the identification of accommodations and modifications for a student to assist in planning for successful general participation in an inclusive setting. The information gathered on the School Participation Checklist may also be incorporated into a student's Measurable Annual Goal.

Individuals with Disabilities Education Act (IDEA), requires that the IEP team identify present level of performance and specific baseline data for each Measurable Annual Goal that is written. To be measurable the baseline must be quantifiable in some way. The data from the School Participation Checklist may be used as baseline data. The School Participation Checklist may be used in a pre- post- assessment format to measure growth. Depending on the type of skill requiring instruction other assessments may also be needed. A task analysis may be needed to determine the steps in a routine and the student's ability to complete each step.

Diane Twachtman-Cullen states in her book, *How Well Does Your IEP Measure Up?* (2000), that the successful performance of any activity is "always contingent upon certain underlying conditions". She points out that this statement is true whether or not the underlying conditions are explicitly stated in the IEP. Underlying conditions may be identified as:

- Whatever the student needs to be present to accomplish the task or learn the skill to the best of his or her ability.
- Statements that are essential to successful programming.
- Statements that are essential to avoid inappropriate programming.
- Statements that ensure consistency of instruction and support across staff, settings, and instructions.

Underlying conditions affect both the staff and the student. Underlying conditions that influence a staff's ability to successfully implement a program are his/her knowledge of the disability and how the disability affects a learner. This is especially true of Autism Spectrum Disorders. The staff must also be knowledgeable of evidence based practices for working with the focus student. The underlying conditions that influence a student's success include prompts given before the task, compensatory strategies to circumvent the deficit area, accommodation, and modifications.

Where do these underlying conditions fit in an IEP? This question is easily answered. An underlying condition may be incorporated into a Measurable Annual Goal with a simple "given statement". If educators write an IEP goal using the following 6 steps they will be set for success!

1. Name the student and date of completion.
2. Make a "given" statement of underlying conditions.
3. Describe the observable behavior.

4. Add clarifying information if necessary.
5. Performance level.
6. Evaluation criteria/measurement.

Examples of "given" statements are:

- Given a trained peer…
- Given a portable visual schedule…
- Given direct instruction…
- Given a list of written rules…
- Given a social script…
- Given more time…

The underlying condition does not address how the goal will be taught or identify a specific methodology. An underlying condition is a description of one or more elements that must be present to ensure successful participation and learning. As previously noted often times the underlying conditions are present without being stated within the IEP goal; however, there is a high likelihood that the underlying conditions will be implemented more consistently if they are included in the IEP goal. Using a completed Accommodation and Modification Planning Form (See Figure 2.a), an educator has a list of underlying conditions that will be of assistance to ensure the success of the student.

Case Study: Teaching Recess

The following Case Study is of a 2nd grade student who is in an inclusive setting for 90% of the day. He is very verbal and enjoys books. He receives speech and language services and resource teacher support on a pull out and in class basis. He is diagnosed with Autism. The following data prompted a request for weekly consultation from a Program Specialist for Autism. The underlying conditions are written in italics in the sample IEP goal.

Baseline Data:

- School Participation Checklist indicated that 80 – 90% of the time he needed support in communication and social skills.
- 50% of the time the student is over focused on one specific peer.
- During 25 minutes of lunch recess there were 9 rough touches and 11 other touches.
- Aggressive touches averaged 2 per day. These were primarily choking and pushing hard.
- Student can take turns when playing a table board game 70% of the time with supervision and prompting from an adult.
- Student engages in turn taking games and reciprocal interactive play in unstructured recess time 0% of the time.

Hypothesis:

The student's deficits in initiation, understanding abstract information (rules of games), perspective taking, and ability to understand reciprocal social interaction promotes and sustains inappropriate initiation by rough touch, choking, and over focus on a single peer. Direct instruction in social interactions is required to replace the inappropriate attempts to initiate play. (See Figures 2.20 and 2.21)

IEP Goal:

By June (one year from today), *given direct instruction, trained peers, and an adult in the vicinity,* the student will develop personal and social skills by initiating a game with a peer, following the established rules and taking 5 turns, 30% of the time 4 out of 5 days as recorded on daily data sheet.

- Met: This Measurable Annual Goal was met and exceed (See Figures 2.22, 2.23, and 2.24).

Objectives:

- By Nov., *given the staff within 3 feet of the student providing prompts from a least to more intrusive level,* the student will ask 2 peers to play a game at recess, learn the rules and sequence for 1 recess game that requires turn taking, by repeating the rules as listed by the peers, he will take turns 4 out of 5 times (80% of the time).

  - Met for catching a ball.

- By March, *given staff within 6 feet proximity,* the student will do the same as above with 2-3 peers, learning 3 additional games and taking turns 10% of the time with .

  - Met at 11% across 3 games.

- By June, *given daily opportunity (5-10 minutes) to participate in a structured game activity at recess with supervision from 20',* the student will generalize the ability to initiate social participation to the playground.

  - Met at 100%.

Program Description

Activity: Playing games with peers at recess.

Approximate Time: 10 -15 minutes daily.

General Procedures: (See Figure 2.20).

- Staff and student decide on a game.

- Student is prompted to ask 1 or 3 friends to play the game.

- Rules are determined.

- Rules and skills are practiced slowly by each student (expert players "average peers" first).

- Turn taking is modeled by each student.

- Verbal commenting is scripted for each student one time by staff.

- Students are given a few minutes to play with staff prompts as needed based on a least to most information hierarchy (See Figure 2.21).

Adult Direction or Action:	**Student Response:**
Offer a choice: (student) what game would you like, kick ball or 2 square?	Student makes a choice.
Who do you want to play with today?	Student names 2 – 3 peers
Find your friends and say, Want to play ___?	Student imitates verbal model
Ask peer, "What are the rules for ____? Then ask student to repeat the rules.	Student imitates verbal model
Ask peer to model skills, cue peer to say your turn to student.	Student imitates skill

Figure 2.20 Specific Adult Actions and Expected Student Responses

General Prompts	Least to Most Prompts	Plan to Fade Prompts
• Verbal script as cue • Peer model • Choices • Staff proximity	• Independent • Peer Model • Peer Verbal • Staff Model • Staff Verbal	• Delay delivery of verbal script • Prepare peers to facilitate activity • Move staff proximity farther away from the activity 3' to 6' or further as appropriate

Figure 2.21 Prompt Hierarchy and Plan to Fade Prompts

Additional Comments:

1. Make games special and fun to entice all to want to participate.

2. Use primary reinforcement or other desired item (stickers, etc.) or another activity of choice at the conclusion of the first game.

3. Send the group off happy with the experience.

4. Allow the game to continue if requested by the group.

Year End Summary Data

The task analysis to teach social interaction at recess listed the following seven steps:

- Choose a game.

- Choose one to three peers.

- Ask the peer/peers to play.

- State the rule.

- Model the rule.

- Imitate the skills to the game.

- Take five turns each.

The steps in this routine broke out into three separate areas (See Figures 2.22, 2.23, and 2.24). The percentages are an average of the steps in each area. The prompt hierarchy range included independent, peer prompted (which was perceived as a naturalized prompt), staff prompt. (See Figure 2.21) The percentages shown are for the independent and peer prompted level.

The final data quantifiably shows that the focus student met and exceeded his Measurable Annual IEP goal. He also eliminated his aggressive behaviors, thus proving the hypothesis correct in that he lacked the ability to initiate and sustain an appropriate interaction with peers. It also must be noted that part of the success of the instruction was due in part to the involvement of the peers who had participated in ability awareness training and were coached in ways to respond to the focus student, assist him in learning the rules of the games, and turn taking skills. More about ability awareness will be presented in Chapter 6.

Steps	Kick Ball	Go Fish	2 Square	Catch	Overall Average
Choose Game Choose Peer	89% independent	75% independent	78% independent	83% independent	81% independent

Figure 2.22 Steps in Task Analysis Teaching Initiation

Ask to play State rule Model rule Imitate skill	41% independent 13% peer prompt	25% independent 6% peer prompt	67% independent 17% peer prompt	30% independent 17% peer prompt	41% independent 13% peer prompt

Figures 2.23 Steps in Task Analysis Teaching Skills and Rules of the Game

Turn #1 #2 #3 #4 #5	18% independent 45% peer prompt	15% independent 70% peer prompt	22% independent 47% peer prompt	40% independent 20% peer prompt	24% independent 46% peer prompt

Figures 2.24 Steps in Task Analysis Teaching Turn Taking

The average percentage across all games and steps in the routine was:

1. 49% of the time independent.
2. 30% of the time peer prompted.
3. 21% of the time staff prompted.

Longitudinal data on this focus student reveals that he has maintained the social skills he learned in 2nd grade. Rough touch has not been a problem and he has maintained and expanded his knowledge of reciprocal games. Although he continues to require instruction in the hidden rules and subtleties of social interaction his general relationships with his peers are positive.

SECTION 7: SUGGESTIONS FOR MEASURABLE ANNUAL IEP GOALS
Ideas across the Age Groups and Skill Categories of the School Participation Checklist

This Section is to provide a team with a framework of ideas from which to generate individualized goals. The goals are presented across the same age groups used on the SPC Preschool – 3d grade (See Figure 2.25), 4th – 8th grade (See Figure 2.26), and 9th – 12th grade (See Figure 2.27), While the suggested goals are not aligned with the state standards, they do relate to many of the core areas that are impaired in individuals on the autism spectrum. Goals must be based on the individual assessed needs of the student and relate directly to the baseline data gathered on the skill. Baseline data will not be presented with these goal ideas.

These goal ideas begin with a given statement of the underlying conditions, shown in italics, that must be in place for the goal to be successfully met.

Sample IEP Goals across Skill Categories

Preschool – 3rd Grade

Skill Category: Patterns of Behavior
Given a visual wait card and direct instruction, the student will wait patiently for his turn (up to 1 minute) independently, by holding his wait card, 4 out of 5 times per day as recorded on his daily data log by staff.
Skill Category: Attending
Given a visual timer and the choice of a preferred activity at the end of the designated work time, the student will stay on task for assigned work task for 3-5 minutes, 4 out of 5 times per day as recorded on his daily data log by staff.
Skill Category: Communication
Given pictures of preferred toys, the student will request a toy from either a peer or adult by handing the picture of the preferred toy to the individual independently in unstructured situations, 4 out of 5 of the appropriate opportunities, per day as recorded on his daily data log by staff.
Skill Category: Social Skills
Given selected average peers and a game chosen from 3 options, rule modifications, and a staff within 3 feet proximity, the student will play a board game by taking 5 to 10 turns and giving a high five at the end of the game independently 40% of the time average for the quarter as recorded by staff in the daily data log.

Figure 2.25

4th – 8th Grade

Skill Category: Patterns of Behavior
Given a visual "to do" list and instruction to use the list, the student will follow the typical class routine of gathering materials for a project by getting each item on her list and checking off the items independently 90% of the time as recorded on the student daily self monitoring checklist
Skill Category: Attending
Given a structured work system with folders to chunk the expected work into manageable pieces and visual information telling him what free choice he can do when he is finished with work, the student will sustain attention to his work and maintain an appropriate working rate by completing all the folders in the to do box and placing them in his finished box then moving on to his choice activity. The student will use the work system independently 100% of the time completing 90-100% of his work as recorded in the teacher's grade book.
Skill Category: Communication
Given topics of interests submitted by his peers and pre-teaching by an adult, the student will identify topics that are of interest to his peers by answering the question, "What do you think Joe wants to talk about today?" with 80% accuracy on 4 out of 5 days as recorded in daily data log.
Skill Category: Social Skills
Given additional visual supports such as white boards in the shape of cartoon communication shapes and a written conversation script, the student will demonstrate how to handle and understand teasing by role playing with familiar adults with 80% accuracy, 4 out of 5 times in a structured situation as recorded by staff in data log.

Figure 2.26

9th – 12th Grades

Skill Category: Patterns of Behavior
Given direct instruction and daily practice on a graphic organizer *that identifies the penalty or bonus for the completion of class* *assignments*, the student will turn in 70% of his assignments on time by learning to prioritizing the sequence of assignments and complete the graphic organizer on a daily basis with 70% accuracy. Teacher grade book will be used to determine mastery.
Skill Category: Attending
Given a simple graphic organizer that chunks information into the key *components and key words from a lecture*, the student will increase her ability to stay focused on the teacher's lecture by filling in missing content on the graphic organizer with 80% accuracy as documented in the student's binder.
Skill Category: Communication
Given written directions that use simple and literal words to accom- *pany a teacher's verbal directions*, the student will increase her ability to the respond to the teacher's directions independently by 50% as recorded in frequency data in student's daily data log.
Skill Category: Social Skills
Given a Venn Diagram and instruction on how to use it to determine *shared interests with friends*, the student will initiate social interaction by starting the interaction based on shared interest identified on the Venn Diagram 90% of the time in structures settings and 45% of the time in unstructured settings as recorded in staff written observation and student self monitoring chart.

Figure 2.27

REFERENCES

American Psychiatric Association. *Diagnostic and Statistical Manual of Mental Disorders Fourth Edition*. Washington, DC: American Psychiatric Association, 1994.

Buron, K. D. and Curtis, M. *The Incredible 5-Point Scale: Assisting Students with Autism Spectrum Disorders in Understanding Social Interactions and Controlling Their Emotional Responses.* Shawnee Mission, KN: Autism Asperger Publishing Company, 2003.

Bondy, A. & Frost, L. *A Picture's Worth: PECS and other visual Communication Strategies in Autism*. Bethesda, MD: Woodbine House, 2002.

Collaborative Workgroup on Autistic Spectrum Disorders. *Best Practices for Designing and Delivering Effective Programs for Individuals With Autistic Spectrum Disorders.* Sacramento, CA: California Department of Education, 1997.

Davies, A. *Teaching Asperger's Students Social Skills Through Acting, All Their World's a Stage!* Arlington, TX: Future Horizons, 2004.

Frost, L. & Bondy, B. *The Picture Exchange Communication System: Training Manual.* Newark, DE: Pyramid Educational Products, Inc., 2002.

Gray, C. *Comic Strip Conversations*. Arlington, TX: Future Horizon, 1994.

Gray, C. Social Stories™ 10.0. *Jenison Autism Journal* Vol.15 #4, 2004.

Gray, C. *The Original Social Stories*. Arlington, TX: Future Horizon, 1993.

Leaf, R. and McEachin, J. *A Work in Progress.* New York, NY: DRL Books, L.L.C., 1999.

Lighthall, K. *What Makes School Great? FRIENDS! Activities to Build Autism Awareness and Develop Friendships.* Redding, CA: Autism and Behavior Training Associates Publications, 2008. www.autismandbehavior.com

Lighthall, K. and Schetter, P. *White Board Words and Thoughts.* Redding, CA: Autism and Behavior Training Associates Publications, 2008. www.autismandbehavior.com

McAfee, J. *Navigation the Social World.* Arlington, TX: Future Horizon, 2002.

Mesibov. G.B., & Howley, M., *Accessing the Curriculum for Pupils with Autistic Spectrum Disorders: Using the TEACCH Programme to Help Inclusion.* London, England: David Fulton Publishers Ltd, 2003.

Mesibov, G.B., Shea, V, & Schopler, E., (2004), *The TEACCH Approach to Autism Spectrum Disorders.* New York, NY: Kluwer Academic/Plenum Publishers, 2004.

Ozonoff, S., Dawson, D., & McPartland. *A Parent's Guide to Asperger Syndrome & High-Functioning Autism.* New York, NY: The Guilford Press, 2002.

Ozonoff, S., Rogers, S., Hendren, R. *Autism Spectrum Disorders: A Research Review for Practitioners.* Arlington, VA: American Psychiatric Publishing. Inc, 2003.

Schetter, P. *Learning the R.O.P.E.S. for Improved Executive Function.* Redding, CA: Autism and Behavior Training Associates Publications, 2004, 2008.

Twachtman-Cullen, D. *How Well Does Your IEP Measure Up?* Higganum, CT: Starfish Specialty Press, 2000.

Wagner, S. *Inclusive Programming for Elementary Students with Autism.* Arlington, TX: Future Horizon, 1999.

Wagner, S. *Inclusive Programming for Middle School Students with Autism/Asperger's Syndrome.* Arlington, TX: Future Horizon, 2002.

Wilde, L., Koegel, L., & Koegel R. *Increasing Success in School Through Priming: A Training Manual.* Santa Barbara, CA: University Of California, Santa Barbara, 1992.

Winner, M. G. *Inside Out: What Makes a Person with Social Cognitive Deficits Tick?* San Jose, CA: Michelle Garcia-Winner Publisher, 2002.

Winner, M. G. *Thinking About You Thinking About Me.* San Jose, CA: Michelle Garcia-Winner Publisher, 2002.

.Wolfberg, P. J. *Peer Play and the Autism Spectrum.* Shawnee Mission, KN: Autism Asperger Publishing Co, 2003.

Wolfberg, P. J. *Play & Imagination in Children with Autism.* New York, NY: Teachers College Press, 1999.

RESOURCES

Patterns of Behavior and Attending

Buron, *K. D. A 5 is Against the Law! Social Boundaries Straight Up!* Shawnee Mission, KN: Autism Asperger Publishing Company, 2007.

Hodgdon, L. *Solving Behavior Problems in Autism (Visual Strategies Series)*, Troy, MI: Quirk Roberts Publishing, 1999.

Koegel, R. and Koegel, L. *Teaching Children with Autism: Strategies for Initiating Positive Interactions and Improving Learning Opportunities.* Baltimore, MD: Paul Brookes Publishing Co, 1996.

Koomar, Kranowits, Szklut, and Balzer-Martin. *Answers to Questions Teachers Ask about Sensory Integration: Forms, Checklists and Practical Tools for Teachers and Parents*. Arlington, TX: Future Horizons Inc. 2001.

Smith-Myles, B., Tapscott-Cook, K., Miller, N., Rinner, L., and Robbins, L. *Asperger's Syndrome and Sensory Issues: Practical Solutions for Making Sense of the World.* Shawnee Mission, KN: Autism Asperger's Publishing Company, 2001.

Smith-Myles, B. and Southwick, J. *Asperger Syndrome and Difficult Moments: Practical Solutions for Tantrums, Rages and Meltdowns,* Shawnee Mission, KN: Autism and Aspergers Publishing, 2005.

Communication

Duke, Nowicki & Martin. *Teaching Your Child the Language of Social Success*, Atlanta, GA: Peachtree Publishers, 1996.

Hodgdon, L. *Visual Strategies for Improving Communication,* Volume 1. Troy, MI: Quirk Roberts Publishing, 1996.

Quill, K. A. *Do-Watch-Listen-Say: Social and Communication Intervention for Children with Autism.* Baltimore MD: Paul H. Brookes Publishing Co, 2000.

Social Skills

Garcia-Winner, Michelle. *Inside Out: What Makes a Person With Cognitive Social Deficits Tick?* San Jose, CA: Michelle Garcia-Winner Publisher, 2000. www.socialthinking.com

Garcia-Winner, M. *Think Social! A Social Thinking Curriculum for School Age Students*. San Jose, CA: Michelle Garcia-Winner Publisher, 2005. www.socialthinking.com

Garcia-Winner, Michelle. *Worksheets for Teaching Social Thinking and Related Skills,* San Jose, CA: Michelle Garcia-Winner Publisher, 2006. www.socialthinking.com

Grandin, T., Barron, S. *Unwritten Super Flex Rules of Social Relationships.* Arlington, TX: Future Horizons Inc. 2001. www.FutureHorizon-autism.com

Gray, C. *Taming the Recess Jungle*. Arlington, TX: Future Horizons Inc. 1993. www.FutureHorizons-autism.com

Madrigal, S. and Garcia-Winner. *Superflex: A Superhero Social Thinking Curriculum.* San Jose, CA: Think Social Publishing, 2008.

Moyes, R. *Incorporating Social Goals in the Classroom: A Guide for Teachers and Parents for Children with High-Functioning Autism and Asperger Syndrome.* London, England: Jessica Kingsley Publishers, 2001. www.jkp.com.

Smith-Myles, Trautman, and Schelvan. *The Hidden Curriculum: Practical Solutions for Understanding Unstated Rules in Social Situations.* Shawnee Mission, KN: Autism Asperger Publishing Company, 2004.

Issues Facing Adolescences with ASD

Bolick, T. *Asperger Syndrome and Adolescence: Helping Preteens and Teens Get Ready for the Real World.* Gloucester, Mass: Fair Winds Press, 2001.

Jackson, L. Freaks, *Geeks, and Asperger Syndrome.* London, England: Jessica Kingsley Publishers, 2002.

Molloy, H. and Vasil, L. *Asperger Syndrome, Adolescence, and Identity: Looking Beyond the Label.* London, England: Jessica Kingsley Publishers, 2004.

Newport, J. and Newport, M. *Autism-Asperger & Sexuality Puberty and Beyond.* Arlington, TX: Future Horizons. Inc., 2002.

Santomauro, J. and Santomauro, D. *Asperger Download: A Guide to Help Teenage Males with Asperger Syndrome Trouble-Shoot Life's Challenges.* Shawnee Mission, KN: Autism and Aspergers Publishing, 2007.

Sicile-Kira, C. *Adolescents on the Autism Spectrum: A Parents Guide to the Cognitive, Social, Physical, and Transition Needs of Teenagers with Autism Spectrum Disorders*. New York, NY: The Berkley Publishing Group, 2006.

Smith-Myles, B. and Adreon, D. *Asperger Syndrome and Adolescence: Practical Solutions for School Success.* Shawnee Mission, KN: Autism and Aspergers Publishing, 2001.

Willey, Liane Holliday. *Asperger Syndrome in Adolescence: Living with the Ups and Downs and Things in Between.* London, England. Jessica Kingsley Publishers, 2003.

CHAPTER 3
R.**E.**A.D.Y.
ENVIRONMENTS FOR INSTRUCTION

Assessing for Environments Success with the V.E.S.T. Checklist

Students with Autism Spectrum Disorders (ASD) present a unique challenge for educators. The life-long neurological impairment is recognized by a triad of impairments in the areas of reciprocal social interaction, communication, and restricted, repetitive behaviors, interests or activities. Mesibov, Shea, and Schopler (2005) note that autism affects all facets of daily life and the way an individual understands the world. They add that people with autism, "tend to be devalued because of their difference." They conclude that although autism is not a culture in the true sense of the word; it does present characteristics and predictable patterns of thinking and behavior in individuals that might be considered the "culture of autism".

It is recognized that there is a broad spectrum of individual differences in people with autism. If one can think of autism as a culture, acknowledging the cultural differences that individuals must deal with on a daily basis, it becomes quite clear that to survive in this world the person with autism or ASD needs help from people who understands the "culture of autism" and can interpret the neuro-typical world to the person with ASD.

Although it is widely acknowledged that there are elements in the environment that may either support or hinder learning for students with ASD there are few tools that assists the educator to systematically evaluate the classroom environment for characteristics that will support students with ASD. One might say that the V.E.S.T. is the best tool to meet this need. (See Figures 3.1 and 3.2) The V.E.S.T. acronym reminds educators of four critical areas to consider and evaluate in the classroom when preparing to teach students with ASD.

1. **Visual** information offered for clarification.

2. **Environmental** and physical structure to clarify expectations.

3. **Structure** that clarifies materials, assignments, and procedures.

4. **Teaching** the obvious skills that are expected of students without direct instruction.

The *V.E.S.T. Checklist* embraces the "culture of autism" by recognizing that educators must accommodate to meet the environmental and learning needs of the students with ASD. The neurological differences which characterize ASD usually prevent the students from accessing typical instruction and learning environments successfully even when the students try very hard to participate. Teachers may use the *V.E.S.T. Checklist* to complete a self evaluation of their classroom environment to determine how to prepare for the arrival of a student with ASD; or how they might improve the environment to address the "culture of autism". *The*

The V.E.S.T. Checklist

Complete this checklist to determine your level of readiness to support the learning of a child with ASD or other developmental delays.

Be VISUAL	Yes	No	Comment/Action
Visually label areas			
Materials are clearly marked			
Classroom schedule is posted			
Schedule changes are visual			
Work stations are labeled			
Boundaries are visual			
Visual cue for transition			
Shelves are clearly labeled			
Important info is highlighted			
Materials are color coded			
Visual cue for waiting			
Reinforcement is visual			
Rules are visual			
Pictures or icons are used			
Teach to look for visual cues			

Learning ENVIRONMENT	Yes	No	Comment/Action
Furniture used to define areas			
Seating for max. focus on task			
Classroom is clutter free			
Distractions are limited (sensory)			
Teacher's desk is out of the way			
Carpets used to filter noise			
Sensory issues reduced			
Quiet "Break Area" provided			
Beanbag chairs in "Break Area"			
Designated transition area			
Furniture is appropriate size			
Materials in designated place			

Figure 3.1 V.E.S.T. Checklist page 1

The V.E.S.T. Checklist

Be STRUCTURED	Yes	No	Comment/Action
Schedule reviewed daily			
Schedule is predictable			
Individual visual schedules			
Sequenced task cards			
Predictable presentation:			
• Left to right			
• Top to bottom			
Staff has instructional plans			
Activities are prepared ahead			
Reinforcement schedules defined			
Reinforcers are assessed regularly			
Data is collected daily			
Program change is based on data			
Consistent prompting is used			
Structured peer play is set up			

TEACH the obvious	Yes	No	Comment/Action
Compliance "Learning to Learn"			
Attention "Learning to Learn"			
Imitation "Learning to Learn"			
Responding to instructions			
Discriminating instructions			
Waiting			
Staying on Task			
Engagement			
Understanding feedback			
Coping with stress			
Coping with loosing/disappointment			
Coping with change			
Playing with toys			
Playing with peers			

Figure 3.2 V.E.S.T. Checklist page 2

V.E.S.T. Checklist (See Figure 3.1 and 3.2) is two pages long and allows the teacher to quickly determine if an element is present or absent from the environment. To complete a *V.E.S.T. Checklist* evaluation of the classroom a teacher simply checks the "Yes" box if the accommodation is in place or "No" if it is not present. A comment should be made if the "No" box is checked to explain why that area is not being addressed. *The V.E.S.T. Checklist* is designed to be thought provoking and might cause an educator to ask the following questions:

Why make the child's world **V**ISUALLY clear?

Making the world visually clear capitalizes on the students' strongest learning modality. Research and clinical literature indicates that most individuals with ASD are better visual learners when compared to their auditory processing of verbal information. (Quill, 1997; Schuler, 1995; Tubbs, 1966). Many individuals with high functioning autism like Temple Grandin Ph.D. (1995) describe her cognitive style as "thinking in pictures". Models such as Treatment and Education of Autistic and related Communication handicapped Children (TEACCH) and Pictures Exchange Communication Systems (PECS) have demonstrated through research the successful use of visual supports in learning many skills. Lynn Hodgdon (1995 & 1999) has written two books about using visual supports to improve communication and behavior. It should also be noted that learning style research indicates that about 40% of all students are visual learners. Keeping that thought in mind educators may feel confident that if they are making the world more visually clear for a student with ASD they are also supporting nearly half of the other students in the class.

What can educators do? Keith Lightbody, an Information and Communication Technology Consultant (2004), suggests fostering "visual literacy" for all learners. He defines visual literacy as, "the ability to understand and produce visual messages." "A visual text makes its meaning with images, or with meaningful patterns and sequences" states Steve Moline on his Visual Literacy K-8 website, (May 2005).

In *The TEACCH Approach to Autism Spectrum Disorders* (2005) Mesibov, Shea, and Schopler state that "three aspects of visual information that help make tasks clear, meaningful and comprehensible are 1) visual instructions; 2) visual organization; and 3) visual clarity."

Visual instructions clarify exactly what is to be done and in what order. It can also teach flexibility because once a person has learned to follow visual instruction most changes are acceptable since the change is just a new part of the instructions. Visual organization helps the person with ASD to focus in on the relevant details; see the task in "chunks" or segments that are understandable; and see predictable patterns that will help them be more organized rather than disorganized and overwhelmed. Visual clarity adds extra information to materials or the environment that will help the person pick out what is important.

Brian Mathis and Jennifer Simmons consultant from the Diagnostic Center North (2007) listed in their workshop *The Eyes Have It: Tapping the Visual Modality to Increase Teaching Effectiveness* the following types of visual supports: 1) demonstrations; 2) models of the finished product; 3) gestures; 4) objects in the environment; 5) arrangement of the environment; 6) pictures; 7) written words (symbols including numbers). They also note that there is a range of visual supports from "No Tech to High Tech" which must be matched to the individual's level of understanding. Some students may require visual supports that are tangible, simple and concrete; whereas other students may successfully use visual information that is representational, complex and more abstract.

A Few Ideas for the Classroom

1. Use photos, line drawings, or icons to:
   - Sequence instructions or group activities.
   - Structure or sequence play activities or routines.
   - Schedule the day for the group and the individual.
   - Clarify expectations (rules) or explain activities.
2. Indicate a change with a visual cue.
   - Use a symbol that is age appropriate and has a positive connotation, such as a happy face, balloon, heart etc.
   - Use the universal no symbol $\oslash$ to indicate what will not occur and place the new event to the right of the deleted event.
3. Organize materials visually.
   - Left to right or top to bottom.

4. Color code or label areas in the room or highlight the information keys on worksheets.
5. Teach children how to look for visual information.
6. Write it down in a list, chart, poster or sign.

Why Think About the ENVIRONMENT?

Understanding the "culture of autism" will reveal several reasons why consideration must be given to the impact the physical environment has on people with ASD. Children with autism are often described as "in their own worlds". They may over-attend to stimuli that is of interest to them but does not clarify expectations of the environment. This is often called stimulus over-selectivity. They may know details but, not know how they fit together or what is expected.

It has also been well established that children with autism have difficulty with their thresholds of sensory input. Sensory input for them is either too much or too little across all the senses. These problems with the control of the sensory input often times maybe resolved by looking at conditions in the person's environments which impact the senses.

Students with ASD are concrete learners. Classrooms and other environments may be ambiguous and abstract, thus not giving the individual adequate information that is concrete enough to know what is expected socially, behaviorally or academically. The results of inadequate information are typically unconventional behavior on the part of the student with ASD. This can easily lead to frustration and confusion for everyone.

What can educators do? The TEACCH model (2005), suggests that the organization and structure of the physical environment should make expectations "clear, interesting, and manageable for individuals with ASD." They also add that "the degree and type of physical organization differs among individuals," thus one must know the unique learning needs of the person with ASD.

The physical organization of the room tells the students what activity occurs in each area by the materials that are present. There needs to be clearly defined boundaries for each activity area. Labels with pictures and or words or color coding may also identify specific areas and clarify expectations. Other considerations may include traffic patterns, proximity to the board, door, restroom, widows to name a few. It is also important to minimize distractions of noise, smell, vision and light which can stimulate sensory overload.

A Few Ideas for the Classroom
1. Create defined areas by the use of:
   - Furniture/dividers.
   - Materials.
   - Lines or footprints on the floor.
   - Carpet squares.
2. Visually indicate where an area or activity begins and ends.
3. Reduce classroom clutter from both staff and students' areas.
4. Organize the classroom to limit sensory over stimulation by using:

- Dividers.
- Light shields (1/3 bulbs covered with soft blue of pink).
- No perfume or other strong fragrances.
- Seat students away from distractions; this needs to be individualized as not all students are distracted by the same things.
- Limit verbal output and provide additional visuals to promote understanding.

Why consider providing greater STRUCTURE?

It is well known within the "culture of autism" that individuals prefer predictable routines. Clear structure provides the predictability that helps children with autism better understand the expectations; remain calm; learn more efficiently; achieve independence; and manage their behavior appropriately to name a few positive outcomes.

What can educators do? There are several things that educators may do, but first and foremost, is to establish positive and predictable daily routines. If a routine is not clear to the student with autism there is a high likelihood that they will create a personal routine. The student's routine may not meet the expectations of the educator. There must be a focus on the relevant information including changes that may occur in the routine. This information must be presented visually. It is important to be consistent with instruction and expectations across staff and environments. Visual schedules, instruction and work routines will support the consistency required for a student with ASD and will support other learners as well. Staff will also benefit from a clearly outlined daily schedule of activities and responsibilities.

Author's Note: Providing an age appropriate daily schedule and teaching the skills for independent use of the schedule are invaluable life skills. Most adults keep some type of planner to organize their life. It is critical to begin the use of a schedule with young children and naturalize the form and content as the student grows.

A Few Ideas for the Classroom

1. Have a visual schedule that is age-appropriate to the student and his needs.
   - Use mini schedules or task cards within activities.
2. Present information in a predictable way.
   - Either left to right or top to bottom.
3. Be visually clear with rules adding pictures for additional emphasis.
4. Use systematic teaching and reinforcement that meets each student's unique needs.
   - Customized prompt hierarchies to the students needs.
   - Use a 3 step prompt method which outlines exactly what information will be given and teach the student the response expectations.
     - Say it (the prompt or instruction) once then move on to the next level of prompt; often times educators repeat a verbal prompt many time even thought the student has not responded appropriately.
5. Set limits in a positive way with visual reminders of what the student is working for; how much time the activity will take; what happen first and what happens next.

6. Offer choices of two things that are acceptable to the staff, not a positive and negative choice, because if the student doesn't make the choice the staff wants the student stills gets the choice he or she made, because it was offered.

Why TEACH the OBVIOUS?

By diagnostic criteria it is known that children with ASD have difficulty understanding and using nonverbal behavior to regulate social interaction. This coupled with other deficits in executive functioning and central coherence prevents students with ASD from learning incidentally. Other research Gaylord-Ross, Haring, Breen & Pitts-Conway 1984: Gena, Krantz, McClannahan, & Poulson, 1996; Koegel, Koegel, & O'Neill, 1989; Ihrig & Wolchik, 1988; Taylor & Harris, 1995) document the profound generalization needs of students with ASD. Twachtman-Cullen and Twachtman-Reilly (2002), state that "students with ASD have deep-seated, systemic problems with generalization that appear to be wired into the disability." Another deficit area for individuals with ASD is Theory of Mind (ToM). It is ToM which allows individuals to successfully take the perspective of others or make inferences about the situation they are experiencing. Simon Baron-Cohn (1997) demonstrated that individuals with ASD perform very poorly on a "false-belief test" which are scenarios designed to measure a person's ability to distinguish between his/her own knowledge about reality and someone else's false belief about reality, in other words, successfully use ToM to interpret a social situation and act upon their beliefs. Given all these issues, one can only imagine how difficult it is for individuals with ASD to interpret the everyday activities of life and respond appropriately.

What can educators do? Summarize all that has been presented before and remember with two critical ideas 1) keep it simple and 2) make it visual. The difficulty here lies in the fact that many of the things that typical children learn at a very early age are social and revolve around play. Educators must continuously remember that play, social skills, and communication require direct instruction in a very simple and visual manner for students with ASD to learn and understand. Most often educators must not only teach the skill but must give the child the words to say. Asking a child with ASD who has a few words to "use your words" may create anxiety rather than the desired social interaction. The older student with ASD may not interpret a situation appropriately and thus, make a social error. Teaching the obvious to most individuals with ASD revolves around socialization because these skills requires the ability to take the perspective of a situation, make inferences, use executive functioning skills and modify one's own behavior to match the situation. Educators must remember that every minute of the school day there are social demands being placed on all students. For a student with ASD to function in school educators must be constantly aware of the importance of teaching more than academics. They must teach the skills that are so obvious to most, but hidden to those with ASD, such as the social skills of being a friend and a student.

A Few Ideas for the Classroom

1. Directly teach skills that may seem obvious to most with a plan:

    *   Play or interaction with a peer whatever the age.

    *   Play with a toy or game.

    *   When a picture is colored and finished.

    *   What to build with blocks.

    *   How to get ready to work.

    *   How to "hang out" with peers.

    *   What to say, do not say, "Use your words," give them the words.

    *   Teach recess (See Chapter 2 Section 6 for a Case Study).

2 Easy and Bright Ideas
Keep it SIMPLE and make it VISUAL!

REFERENCES

Baron-Cohen, S. *Mindblindness an Essay on Autism and Theory of Mind.* Cambridge, MA: The MIT Press, 1997.

Frost, L. & Bondy, B. T*he Picture Exchange Communication System: Training Manual.* Newark, DE: Pyramid Educational Products, Inc., 2002.

Frith, U. *Autism Explaining the Enigma.* Ontario UK: Blackwell Publishing,1989 and 2003.

Gaylord-Ross, R. J., Haring, T. J., Breen, C., & Pitts-Conway, V. The training and generalization of social interaction skills with autistic youth. *Journal of Applied Behavior Analysis,* 17(2), 229-247. 1984.

Grandin, T. *Thinking in Pictures: And other reports from my life with autism.* New York, NY: Random House, 1995.

Gena, A., Krantz, P.J., McClannahan, L. D., & Poulson, C.L. Training and generalization of affective behavior displayed by youth with autism. *Journal of Applied Behavior Analysis,* 29(3), 291-304. 1996.

Hodgdon, L.A. *Visual Strategies for Improving Communication: Practical Supports for School and Home.* Troy, MI: QuirkRoberts, 1995.

Hodgdon, L.A. *Solving Behavior Problems In Autism: Improving Communication With Visual Strategies.* Troy MI: QuirkRoberts, 1999.

Ihrig, K. and Wolchik, S. A. Peer versus Adult Models and Autistic Children's Learning: Acquisition, Generalization, And Maintenance. *Journal of Autism and Developmental Disorders,* 18(1), 67-69. 1988.

Koegel, R. L., Koegel, L. K., & O'Neill, R. Generalization in the treatment of autism. In L. V. McReynolds & J.E. Sprandlin (Eds.), *Generalization strategies in the treatment of communication disorders* (pp. 116-131). Toronto: BC: Decker, 1989.

Lightbody, K. *Visual Literacy in Classrooms.* 2007. http://www.zardec.net.au/keith/visual.htm

Mesibov, G.B., Shea, V., and Schopler, E. *The TEACCH Approach to Autism Spectrum Disorders.* New York, NY: Kluwer Academic /Plenum Publishers, 2005.

Moline, Steve. *Visual Literacy K-8,* http:www//k-8visual.info, 2005

Schreibman, L. *The Science and Fiction of Autism.* Cambridge, MA: Harvard University Press, 2005.

Schuler, A. L. Thinking in autism: Differences in learning and development. Un K.A. Quill (Ed.), *Teaching children with autism: Strategies to enhance communication and socialization* (pp. 11-32). New York, NY: Delmar, 1995.

Quill, K. Instructional considerations for young children with autism: The rationale for visually cued instructions. *Journal of Autism and Developmental Disorders,* 21, 697-714. 1997.

Taylor, B. A., & Harris, S. L. Teaching children with autism to seek information: Acquisition of novel information and generalization of responding. *Journal of Applied Behavior Analysis,* 28(1), 3-14. 1995.

Tubbs, V. K. Types of linguistic disability in psychotic children. *Journal of Mental Deficiency Research,* 10, 230-240, 1966.

Twachtman-Cullen, D. & Twachtman-Reilly, J. *How Well Does Your IEP Measure Up?* Higganum, CT, Starfish Specialty Press, LLC, 2002.

RESOURCES FOR SCHEDULES

http://card.ufl.edu/visual.htm

- Where to begin with Visual Supports

www.dotolearn.com

- This site has many ready-made visuals which are easy to print and use
- Overview of making a schedule
- "Make-A-Schedule": online subscription $49.95 per year
- CD $59.95

www.sesa.org/Resources/VisualSchedules/

- Combining Visual Schedules with Mini-Picture Communication Boards

www.cesa7.k12.wi.us/sped/autism/structure/str11.htm

- Visual Schedules and supports related to children with Autism

www.cesa7.k12.wi.us/sped/autism/index2.htm

- Autism intervention strategies including communication, schedules

Other Resources

www.teacch.com

- University of North Carolina website that offer information and product recommendation for TEACCH

CHAPTER 4

R.E.**A.**D.Y.
ACCOMMODATING FOR LEARNING DIFFERENCES

A planning form which will assist in identifying expected outcomes, academic accommodations and modifications along with a system for data collection

When a team is preparing for an inclusive education setting they must ask two questions. First, can the student participate in the same manner as the other general education students? If the answer to this question is no, then the second question is what accommodations or modifications are needed?

As stated in Chapter 2, the terms accommodations and modifications must be clearly defined and understood by the team. In review, it is recognized that *accommodations* are changes made within the classroom which provide access for a student with a disability to participate in the general education curriculum which *do not fundamentally alter or lower the standard or expectation* of content mastery. Basic accommodations include changes in quantity, time, input, output, participation and level of support. Each of these areas should be individualized for each student.

Modifications are changes in the classroom instruction or expectations, which may appear to be similar to accommodations but which *do fundamentally alter or lower the standard or expectations* of the instructional objectives of the activities. Basic modifications may include level of difficulty, alternate goals, or a substitute curriculum. These modifications will be individualized based on assessed needs as outlined in the student's IEP.

It is the IEP team's decision based on present levels, special factors, IEP goals, services and setting for the implementation of goals which specific accommodations and modifications would be appropriate for a student. If the IEP team has determined that the general education classroom is the appropriate setting in which to implement the student's goals then the intended overall performance outcomes and expectations in the general education setting should also be determined and documented on the IEP. Identifying which of the following statements best describe the purpose for implementing IEP goals in a general education setting will assist the team in selecting the most appropriate interventions, supports, accommodations and/or modifications for a student with ASD or other disabilities.

The intended outcome is:

- Exposure to general education, to assist in development of positive peer interaction, and to improve social skills and adaptive behavior.

- To gain academic competence in general education curriculum and to participate, as appropriate, in learning activities (with modifications and accommodations as necessary).

- To perform most class activities and assignments and to obtain optimal grade level curriculum mastery (accommodations as necessary).

- That the student **is expected** to meet the same standards of curriculum content mastery as the students not receiving special education services within the classroom.
  - Mastery may be demonstrated with accommodations
  - Grading is the responsibility of the general education teacher
  - Consultation is available from the special education teacher
- That the student **is not** expected to meet the same standards of curriculum mastery as the students not receiving special education services in the same class.
  - The student will require modifications and accommodations
  - Grading will be collaboratively accomplished between the general education and special education teachers
  - Grades will be modified in accordance with the district policy

An IEP team is required by law to indicate supplemental supports, including accommodations and modifications, on the IEP document. The law also requires that the public agency shall ensure that *all educators or others* providing services to the student are informed of their specific responsibilities in the implementation of the identified accommodations and modifications. To meet this mandate the *Accommodation and Modifications Planning Form* (See Figure 4.1) was developed.

Frequently there is not adequate space on the IEP document to list all the specific supports and how the professionals who are responsible for the implementation might accomplish this goal. This *Accommodation and Modification Planning Form* is not an official IEP document; however it may be attached to an IEP to provide a more detailed description of what specifically will be provided for the student.

Additional uses for the *Accommodation and Modification Planning Form* included the following:

- Establishing collaboration between the general educator and special educator.
- Planning for an IEP meeting.
- A clear and visually way to share information at an IEP meeting.
- A simple way for the parents to review teacher recommendations and add their suggestions either before of during the IEP meeting.
- Assist in developing a shared vision of the expected outcomes for the student while participating in the general education classroom.

When considering the best practices for accommodations and modifications one must remember the following:

- The IEP team identifies the needed accommodations and modifications.
- The accommodations and modifications must always be included in the IEP document.
- They are implemented collaboratively by all the designated service providers.
- Data is recorded to determine if the accommodations and modifications are successfully supporting the student.

ACCOMMODATION AND MODIFICATION PLANNING FORM

Student:	Grade/Class(es):	Date:

Team developing the plan:

Persons responsible for implementation:

This form is to assist a team in planning supports for inclusive settings. Prior to completing this form mark the following statements that best describes the intended outcomes and expectations for the student. These statements will assist the team in determining whether accommodations and/or modifications are required.

PART 1: Select up to **2 statements** that best describe the desired outcomes.

1. ☐ To be exposed to the general education setting, to assist in development of positive peer interaction; to improve social skills and adaptive behavior.
2. ☐ To gain academic competence in general education curriculum and to participate, as appropriate, in learning activities (with *modifications* and *accommodations* as necessary).
3. ☐ To perform most class activities and assignments and to obtain optimal grade level curriculum mastery (with *accommodations* as necessary).

PART 2: Select **1 statement** that best describe the expectations for participation.

1. ☐ The student **is expected to meet the same standards** of curriculum content mastery and participate in the same manner as non- special education students within the classroom.
   - Mastery may be demonstrated with *accommodations*
   - Grading is the responsibility of the general education teacher
   - Consultation is available from the special education teacher
2. ☐ The student **is not expected** to meet the same standards of curriculum mastery or participate at the same level as non-special education students within the same classroom.
   - The student will require *modifications* and *accommodations*
   - Grading will be collaboratively accomplished between the general education and special education teachers
   - Grades will be modified in accordance with the district policy

PART 3: Possible Accommodations	Specifics for Individualized Student Plan
Input: ☐ Provide additional or modified visual aids ☐ Provide additional written directions, notes etc. ☐ Provide taped books or materials ☐ Use additional manipulative, hands-on activities ☐ Provide concrete examples (visual and/or kinesthetic) ☐ Increased use of cooperative or peer learning groups ☐ Provide discussion notes, outlines etc. ☐ Other:	
Output ☐ Allow verbal rather than written responses ☐ Allow written rather than verbal responses ☐ Demonstrate knowledge through alternative means such as hands-on projects, video report or assignments ☐ Provide for tape recorded assignments ☐ Allow for computer completed assignments ☐ Take tests in alternative setting ☐ Evaluate using alternative means ☐ Other:	

Figure 4.1 Page 1

Possible Accommodations	Specifics for Individualized Student Plan
Quantity: ☐ Shorten task or assignments: less items ☐ Assign only some of the generally required tasks ☐ Learns only key concepts ☐ Provide credit for portion of work completed ☐ Reduce homework ☐ Eliminate homework ☐ Other: ☐ Other:	
Time: ☐ Give additional work time to complete task ☐ Require less time to work on frustrating tasks ☐ Give more frequent breaks from work ☐ Provide a visual method to segment time ☐ Do not require timed testing situations ☐ Other: ☐ Other:	
Level or Type of Participation: ☐ Responds verbally with group ☐ Responds with a gesture ☐ A written response on a white board is held up ☐ Paired partner response or instruction ☐ Written response on paper ☐ Responds after peer models response ☐ Practices response with peer or small ☐ Uses graphic organizers for responses and presentation ☐ Completes a project to demonstrate mastery ☐ Other: ☐ Other:	
Level of Support: ☐ Have student work cooperatively with peers ☐ Assign a cross-age tutor or peer tutor ☐ Provide extra help from teacher or other adult ☐ Implement Behavior Support Plan ☐ Send home daily or weekly progress reports ☐ Set up regular progress conferences with student ☐ Provide daily assignment sheet ☐ Make regularly scheduled home contacts ☐ Other: ☐ Other:	
Additional Considerations: ☐ Special seating arrangement ☐ After school assistance ☐ Develop a menu of positive reinforcers and plan for systematic use ☐ Set up a token economy for reinforcement ☐ Set up a special study/ work area or study carrel ☐ Teach and practice school and or class rules ☐ Modify classroom rules with a written plan ☐ Other: ☐ Other:	

Figure 4.1 Page 2

PART 4: Possible Modification	Specifics for Individualized Student Plan
Difficulty: ☐ Use calculator or computer for assistance ☐ Open book or notes during tests ☐ Simplified assignments and/or materials ☐ Employ lesser performance and evaluation standards ☐ Modify rule and other expectations ☐ Use alternative learning materials in the same content area ☐ Evaluate progress based on alternative means ☐ Other: ☐ Other:	
Alternate Goals: ☐ Identify alternate curriculum goals assigning work and evaluating accordingly with collaboration between general and special educators ☐ Focus on IEP goals using general education activities and a means of meeting the goals ☐ Other: ☐ Other:	
Substitute Curriculum: ☐ Curriculum is completely different from peers ☐ Substitute curriculum developed and implemented primarily by general education teacher ☐ Substitute curriculum developed by special educator and implemented primarily by general education teacher ☐ Curriculum developed and implemented collaboratively by general and special education teachers	

Figure 4.1 Page 3

The *Accommodations and Modifications Planning Form* is divided into four parts. The form begins with basic information about the student and the critical information of who has developed the plan and who the implementers are. As started earlier all providers and educators must be informed of their responsibilities to implement all accommodations and modifications.

Part 1 and Part 2 should be discussed by parents and professionals during the IEP meeting. The selections made in these two parts clarify the overall vision of the team regarding the outcomes and expectations the team shares for the student. Part 1 asks the team to select up to two statements that best describe the expected outcome. The first statement listed reflects the goal of social interaction with peers. In some situations this may be the only expected outcome for the student based on the student's cognitive abilities that are affecting learning. If this is the case then only one of the three statements would be checked and the team could move on the Part 2. However, if the expected student outcome is to engage in the academic curriculum either statement two or three will need to be check. Statement two describes a student who will require both modifications and accommodation, thus indicating that not all academic work will be at the same grade level as the other students in the class. Statement three indicates that the student requires only accommodations, therefore the student is working at grade level with adjustments made to just to reduce the barriers to learning the material and demonstrating mastery that are caused by the disability.

In summary of Part 1, a team may check up to a total of two boxes. Typically statement one is checked for most students. Next the team must select either statement two or three. The team must choose between either statements two or three because the intended outcome is different in each statement.

Part 2 asks the team to determine the expected level of mastery and participation towards meeting the standard for the grade level. In Part 2 the team must choose only one statement that best describes the students expected level of participation. If statement one is chosen then the team is acknowledging that the student is held accountable to the same standard as his or her peers with accommodations only. The general educator takes the lead role in the implementation of the accommodations and grading of the student. Occasionally general educators may feel concerned that they do not have the skills to accommodate instruction for a student with an IEP. However, this typically a semantics issues, as general educators have been implementing "differential instruction" which is really the general education term for accommodations. General educators may not be giving themselves credit for the many accommodations that they are already implementing. Given "Response to Intervention" (RTI) and the overall move to address all learners' individual needs in the general education setting, more and more strategies and methods are available to the general educator.

If statement two is chosen then the team is acknowledging that the student will not be held accountable to the same standard as his or her peers. The student may receive accommodations, but will also receive modifications which will lower the standard of mastery. This student's program is typically highly individualized. It will be created and graded collaboratively by both the general and special educators. Checking this statement does not diminish the value of the student's participation in the class, it simply identifies the overall expectations. Given the pressures of high stakes testing for students, checking this statement may reduce the anxiety level of the general educator who feels the responsibility to have every student in class meet the same standard.

An additional long term implication of a modified program, even if the student is in an inclusive setting, is the issue of earning a high school diploma. Receiving a diploma is based on either district or state requirements. It is recommended that when a student has required a modified curriculum, the IEP team discuss graduation requirement at the transition IEP meeting to high school and determine if a diploma or other recognition, such as a certificate of completion will be earned.

Part 3 lists the six typical areas for accommodations as identified by Diana Browning-Wright (2005). The six areas include input, output, quantity, time, participation, and level of support. The column on the right lists each of these areas with a checklist of possible accommodations that might be included in the respective area. This is not an all inclusive list and educators and IEP teams are encouraged to add ideas that work for each student. The column on the right provides space for the educators or team to briefly describe how this accommodation would be specifically implemented for the student.

The area of input and output are intentionally listed first and second under accommodations because, as the literature reveals, these are the two elements most critical in effective instruction for any student. Acknowledging this, and recognizing that the accommodation is used to circumvent the student's learning differences or deficits that cause barriers to learning, it is vitally important that the team closely attend to the input and output accommodations. In short the team must identify how the educator is going to present that material in a way the student can learn it and how the student can demonstrate that the material has been learned.

Input and output both could be classified under the heading of communication. Given that one of the core deficit areas for a student with ASD is communication it becomes even more vital that these areas are accommodated. Understanding that the student with ASD, who may happen to have a high vocabulary, still has difficulty with other aspects of communication and language will help in selecting the accommodations that best meets the student's unique needs.

Consideration for the accommodation of quantity requirements is the next area on the planning form. Some students with ASD or other disabilities may require little accommodation in this area; however there are those individuals who may be totally overwhelmed when presented with a full page of math problems, instructed to write a ten page report, or given lengthy verbal directions outlining an assignment. As with all accommodations the quantity of materials and instruction presented or output required must also be individually determined. Some students may require a significant accommodation in one subject area and not in another. Again this is really an issue of input and output, or communication. The team must ask the questions how much can the student take in at one time and what is a reasonable expectation for output, while maintaining the integrity of the content presented?

Time is the next area to be addressed. The pressure of a "timed" test may cause significant anxiety for a student with ASD, as many have reported that it takes them longer to process information. The literature reports that students with ASD have issues with their working memory and when time limits are enforced their ability to recall and restate information they have learned may become very challenging. If the quantity of the output has not been accommodated they may need more time; however if the quantity has been accommodated the student may be expected to complete the assignment within the designated time frame. The student may become overwhelmed with a project as a whole because he or she does not have a concept of how much time a large project might take to complete. In this situation an appropriate accommodation would be teaching the student to "guesstimate" the amount of time required for each part of the project and scheduling the project over the entire time allowed to complete the project. Excellent procedures and visual organizers to teach time management are presented in *Learning the R.O.P.E.S. for Improved Executive Functioning* (Schetter 2004, 2008). Once again, any accommodations to the requirement of time are an IEP team decision based on the individual needs of the student.

Participation of the student in class may be accommodated in terms of level and type. Some students may participate in a manner that is very similar to all the other students in the class while others may feel extremely uncomfortable with expected levels of participation or "output". Appropriate participation in class requires both communication skills, as well as social skills which are both core deficits for students with ASD. For the highly verbal student who tends to blurt out answers because he is fearful someone may steal his answer or he may forget it, a written answer on a white board that may be held up for a quick teacher response might accommodate the situation. If the student has difficulty responding in a large group, paired student to student response might be helpful; or only being called on after several students have model the appropriate response. It must be recognized that for students with ASD the social and communication skills required to participate in a classroom may require direct instruction along with the accommodations.

Addressing the Level of Support provided to the student who is in an inclusive setting is the final accommodation listed on this planning form. Additional support may be delivered in a variety of ways including peer tutoring, a buddy system, additional time from educators, regular communication with home or the student, a behavior support plan, and or other visual or structural supports in the educational setting to name a few. Some individuals may think that additional support always means placing an additional staff member in the inclusive setting. This might be the decision that the IEP team makes and this could be noted on this planning form; however it is not the only way to increase support in an inclusive setting. A procedure to assess for the need of an additional staff will be discussed in Chapter 5.

In concluding the discussion of accommodations one must acknowledge that when an accommodation is implemented in a classroom, the compensatory skills needed to eventually use the accommodation independently must be also be taught.

Using a graphic organizer to categorize information is a helpful visual method to accommodate input from a lecture. The ultimate goal of this accommodation would be for the student to have the skills to independently create a graphic organizer to take notes from a lecture or text and organize information in a meaningful way.

For many students with ASD accommodations will never be faded, as they provide the important visual and organization structure needed by the individual to function independently. However, the accommodation will be naturalized and become a way of life. A prime example of this is learning to use a schedule. This is a critical life skill for everyone, but especially for those lacking in organizational skills. When a daily routine is clear for an individual with ASD there is less anxiety and an increased level of independence in moving through the daily routine. A preschool student may begin with a three dimensional object schedule and move on to a two dimensional photograph schedule as his or her understanding grows. As the student becomes competent with one type of schedule it is not faded but naturalized to the next level until in high school the student can independently schedule activities in a planner or a personal technology device. The student who has received the accommodation of a schedule and taught the compensatory skills to use it has a life skill that will provide support at home, in the community, and the workplace.

The reader is reminded that accommodations are put in place to circumvent the barriers to learning that a student experiences when there is an identified deficit. It is the responsibility of the IEP team to recognize what accommodations are required and not just put them in place, but teach the student the compensatory skills to eventually use the accommodation independently. Planning for accommodations will require more than just listing them on the IEP or this form.

Part 4 lists the basic modifications that an educator or IEP team might consider for a student in an inclusive situation. There are four areas in this section including difficulty, alternate goals, and alternate curriculum. The section for additional consideration could be applicable to a student with either accommodations or modifications. By definition a modification lowers the level of difficulty of the skills presented. Thus, a common modification is to have a student placed in an age-appropriate classroom but assigned academic tasks that are one or more grade levels below the class level. The student may also have any or all areas of accommodation with input and output given careful consideration. A student who is having the level of academic difficulty reduced may follow the typical daily schedule for all student's in his or her class, so when the class is working on math the student with the modification is also working on math. The only difference is that the level of difficulty for math has been reduced.

Specific IEP goals typically make up the curriculum requirements for the student with modifications. The student may have an IEP goal in math to make purchases using the "dollar more strategy" which is completely different than any of the grade level math standards. The student may work with material appropriate to this goal during the regular math time. Experiential situations may be set up within or outside the classroom to assist the student in learning these math skills.

If the student does not have an IEP goal in the area of math then when the class is working on math the student will be working on an alternate curriculum goal. Often the alternate curriculum goals are based on functional life skills. For example if the alternate curriculum goal is in the area of social skills the student may have the job of materials monitor and be learning to give eye contact, respond to requests, and hand out materials to students.

The *Additional Considerations* area on the *Accommodations and Modifications Planning Form* lists other types of accommodations that might be discussed by an IEP. They include environmental, motivational, and behavioral considerations. It is recognized that the structure of the environment can significantly influence learning and attention, especially for students with ASD. It is also reported that while students with ASD may appear to be unmotivated, what is true is that they are just differently motivated. Acknowledging these two points may encourage the IEP team to address the items listed under Additional Considerations as possible accommodations.

Once the IEP team has identified the accommodations and/or modifications that are appropriate for the students the educators may choose to use the *R.E.A.D.Y. Matrix for Accommodations and Modifications* as shown in Figure 4.2 to determine which periods of the day the identified accommodations and/or modifications would be most helpful. This form is also very helpful for the paraprofessional. If they are unsure of the type of accommodation or modification during a specific activity, a glance at this simple one page form will give them the answer they need. This gives the new or untrained paraprofessional the information they need without talking to the educator. The trained paraprofessional may feel more confident as they implement the educator's plan for the student. This form also points out the frequency that some accommodation and modifications require. Basically it takes the any guesswork out of the implementation of a plan.

If the educators feel that the accommodations and/or modifications will be used throughout the entire day the educators may want to move directly to the *Accommodations and*

R.E.A.D.Y. MATRIX for ACCOMMODATIONS AND MODIFICATIONS

Student: *Sara Needs*   Date: *November, 2008*   Grade: *3rd*

Directions: Insert a (✓) when there is an opportunity to use the accommodation and or modifications within the daily schedule. Use the information gathered on this form to plan for the consistent use of the identified accommodations and modifications across the day.

Classroom Schedule

Activity, Period or Scheduled Time / A: Accommodations M: Modifications (delete the A /M not used)	Turn in homework	Flag Salute	Journal Write	Reading Workbook	Reading Lg. Group	Social Studies	RECESS	Accelerated Math	Saxon Math	LUNCH	Music	Art	PE
A: Quantity of some work adjusted to task			✓	✓	✓	✓		✓	✓		✓	✓	✓
A: Provide additional visual aids	✓		✓	✓	✓	✓		✓	✓		✓	✓	✓
A: Additional hands-on manipulatives								✓	✓				
A: Provide more concrete examples			✓	✓	✓	✓	✓	✓	✓			✓	
A: Require different and less homework	✓			✓	✓	✓		✓	✓				
A: Homework "priming" for future class lessons				✓	✓	✓		✓	✓				
A: Give more frequent breaks from work			✓	✓	✓	✓		✓	✓		✓	✓	✓
A: Allow verbal rather than written response				✓	✓	✓			✓				
A: Provide extra help from teacher or other adult			✓	✓	✓	✓		✓	✓				
A: Provide extra help from peer or classmate		✓				✓				✓	✓	✓	✓
A: Provide menu of reinforcers	✓	✓	✓	✓	✓	✓	✓	✓	✓	✓	✓	✓	✓
A: Use token economy	✓	✓	✓	✓	✓	✓	✓	✓	✓	✓	✓	✓	✓
A: Implement Positive Behavior Plan	✓	✓	✓	✓	✓	✓	✓	✓	✓	✓	✓	✓	✓
A: Teach and practice rules with visuals	✓	✓	✓	✓	✓	✓	✓	✓	✓	✓	✓	✓	✓
A: Special work area and seating (used daily)			✓	✓	✓	✓		✓	✓		✓	✓	
M: Alternate curriculum and curricular goals			✓	✓	✓	✓	✓	✓	✓	✓	✓	✓	✓
M: Evaluate using alternative means			✓	✓	✓	✓		✓	✓		✓	✓	✓
M: Use alternative learning materials			✓	✓	✓	✓		✓	✓		✓	✓	✓

Comments: Accommodation: *Regular team meeting is held every Tuesday morning for 20 minutes*

Figure 4.2

Modifications Classroom Data Collection Sheet (See Figure 4.3). This simple data collection form provides space to note whether an accommodation or modification was used during the day. The column on the left lists the accommodations and modifications in no particular order. The form provides twenty-one additional columns to be dated in the top row for the consecutive school days in the month. Any staff member may put a check in the box under the date when the accommodation or modification was used.

At the end of the month the educator can tell at one glance, which accommodations or modifications were used consistently and which was not used with regularity. Recognizing that as educators we are striving to teach independence it is important to take data on the frequency that the accommodations and modifications are used. Also remembering that many of the accommodations need to be naturalized while teaching the student the compensatory skills to either request a specific type of support or self-initiate the use of the accommodation (e.g. independently using a graphic organizer to take note in class or from text).

It must be noted that some of the accommodations that students with an IEP may require to be successful in the general education classroom are not considered acceptable in some standardize testing situations. To determine whether an accommodation is accepted as standard or non-standard by a test publisher, it is suggested that the reader review each

ACCOMMODATIONS AND MODIFICATIONS
Classroom Data Collection Sheet

Student: Sara Needs   Month/Year: November, 2008   Grade: 3rd   Teacher: Ms. Cando

List Accommodation and/or Modification in column. Indicate an (A) for accommodation and (M) for modification

Date:	1	2	3	4	5	8	9	10	11	12	15	16	17	19	20	23	24	25	26	27	30
Alternate curriculum and curricular goals M	✓	✓	✓	✓	✓	✓	✓	✓	✓	✓	✓	✓	✓	✓	✓	✓	✓	✓	✓	✓	✓
Quantity of some work adjusted to task. A	✓	✓	✓	✓	✓	✓	✓	✓	✓	✓	✓	✓	✓	✓	✓	✓	✓	✓	✓	✓	✓
Use alternative learning materials as needed M	✓		✓	✓	✓		✓		✓	✓	✓	✓	✓	✓	✓		✓		✓	✓	✓
Provide additional visual aids A	✓	✓	✓	✓	✓	✓	✓	✓	✓	✓	✓	✓	✓	✓	✓	✓	✓	✓	✓	✓	✓
Additional hands-on manipulatives A	✓	✓	✓	✓	✓	✓	✓	✓	✓	✓	✓	✓	✓	✓	✓	✓	✓	✓	✓	✓	✓
Provide more concrete examples A	✓	✓	✓	✓	✓	✓	✓	✓	✓	✓	✓	✓	✓	✓	✓	✓	✓	✓	✓	✓	✓
Require different and less homework A	✓				✓				✓				✓								✓
Homework "priming" for future class lessons A	✓				✓				✓				✓								✓
Give more frequent breaks from work A		✓	✓	✓				✓	✓	✓		✓		✓	✓					✓	✓
Allow verbal rather than written response A		✓					✓					✓		✓			✓		✓		✓
Evaluate using alternative means M				✓					✓					✓						✓	
Provide extra help from teacher or other adult A	✓	✓	✓	✓	✓	✓	✓	✓	✓	✓	✓	✓	✓	✓	✓	✓	✓	✓	✓	✓	✓
Provide menu of reinforcers A	✓						✓	✓	✓									✓			
Use token economy (for selected work) A	✓	✓	✓	✓	✓	✓	✓	✓	✓	✓	✓	✓	✓	✓	✓	✓	✓	✓	✓	✓	✓
Regular team meetings A		✓						✓					✓					✓			
Implement Positive Beh. Intervention Plan A	✓	✓	✓	✓	✓	✓	✓	✓	✓	✓	✓	✓	✓	✓	✓	✓	✓	✓	✓	✓	✓
Teach and practice rules with visuals A	✓	✓	✓	✓	✓	✓	✓	✓	✓	✓	✓	✓	✓	✓	✓	✓	✓	✓	✓	✓	✓
Special work area and seating (used daily) A	✓	✓	✓	✓	✓	✓	✓	✓	✓	✓	✓	✓	✓	✓	✓	✓	✓	✓	✓	✓	✓

Comments:

Figure 4.3

testing manual. Each state typically also has its own guidelines for acceptable accommodations and modifications on state tests. The reader must refer to the individual state's website to determine the approved guidelines.

In summary, accommodations and modifications are mandated by law for students who have been found eligible for special education services. They are identified by the IEP team and noted in the IEP document. All staff working with the student are responsible for implementing the accommodations and modifications as describe in the IEP. However, an important part that should not be overlooked is the student's role. Educators and parents must help the student understand his or her disability and need for the accommodations or modifications. They must teach the student not only how to independently use the accommodations, but how to self advocate for them and why they need to. As students begin to participate in their IEP meetings and plan for transitions to middle school, high school, and beyond it is vital for the students to know what must be in place to ensure their success. College counselors state that one of the most important skills a student should have when leaving high school is the skill to self advocate for the accommodations that circumvent his or her barriers to learning. Many resources on transition and individuals with ASD have been listed at the end of this chapter. A sample letter from a young man with autism to his university requesting specific accommodations is one of the resources.

REFERENCES

Schetter, P. *The R.O.P.E.S. for Improving Executive Functioning Skills in Students with High Functioning Autism and Asperger Syndrome,* Redding, CA: ABTA Publications, 2004 & 2008.

Twachtman-Cullen, D. & Twachtman-Reilly, J. *How Well Does Your IEP Measure Up?* Higganum, CT: Starfish Specialty Press, LLC. 1998.

Wright, D. B. *Teaching and Learning Training. Positive Environments, Network of Trainers,* California Department of Education: Diagnostic Center, South. www.pent.ca.gov 2005.

RESOURCES

Cohen, M. J. and Sloan, D. L. *Visual Supports for People with Autism: A Guide for Parent's and Professionals.* Bethesda, MD: Woodbine House, 2007.

Fein, D. and Dunn, M. A. *Autism in Your Classroom: A General Education's Guide to Students with Autism Spectrum Disorders,* Bethesda, MD: Woodbine House, 2007.

Kluth, P. and Chandler-Olcott, K. *"A Land We Can Share": Teaching Literacy to Students with Autism.* Baltimore, MD: Paul H. Brookes Publishing Co. 2008.

Loomis, D. and Kolberg, K. *The Laughing Classroom: Everyone's Guide to Teaching Humor and Play.* Novato, CA: New World Library, 1993.

Notbohm, E. *Ten Things Your Student with Autism Wishes You Knew*. Arlington, TX: Future Horizons Inc. 2006.

Ozonoff, S., Dawson, G. & McPartland, J. *A Parent's Guide to Asperger Syndrome & High-Functioning Autism.* New York, NY: Guilford Press, 2002.

Silverman, S. M. and Weinfeld. *School Success for Kids with Asperger's Syndrome.* Waco, TX: Prufrock Press Inc. 2007.

Snaver, J. L. and Myles, B. *Making Visual Supports: Work in the Home and Community: Strategies for Individuals with Autism and Asperger Syndrome.* Shawnee Mission, KA: Autism Asperger Publishing Company, 2000.

Sutton, J. D. *101 Ways to Make Your Classroom Special.* Pleasanton, TX: Friendly Oaks Publications, 1999.

Wagner, S. *Inclusive Programming for Elementary Student's with Autism.* Arlington, TX: Future Horizons Inc. 1998, 1999.

Wagner, S. *Inclusive Programming for Middle School Student's with Autism/Asperger's Syndrome.* Arlington, TX: Future Horizons Inc. 2002.

Adolescence with ASD and Transition Needs

Baker, Jed. *Preparing for Life: The Complete Guide for Transitioning to Adulthood for those with Autism and Asperger's Syndrome.* Arlington TX: Future Horizons Inc., 2005. www.FHautism.com

Grandin, T. and Duffy, K. *Developing Talents: Careers for Individuals with Asperger Syndrome and High-Functioning Autism.* Shawnee Mission, KS: Autism Asperger Publishing Company, 2004.

Harpur, Lawlor and Fitagerald. *Succeeding in College with Asperger Syndrome: A Student Guide*. London, England: Jessica Kingsley Publishers, 2004.

Korin, E.S. *Asperger Syndrome: An Owner's Manual 2 for Older Adolescents and Adults*. Shawnee Mission, KN: Autism and Aspergers Publishing, 2007.

Meyer, Rodger. *Asperger Syndrome Employment Workbook*. London. England: Jessica Kingsley Publishers, 2001.

Shore, Stephen (editor). *Ask and Tell: Self-Advocacy and Disclosure for People on the Autism Spectrum*. Shawnee Mission, KS: Autism Asperger Publishing Company, 2004.

Websites

Accommodations letter from a University student with Autism

http://websyr.edu/~jisincla/accommod.htm

Learning Strengths Seminars

www.pent.ca.gov

List of Typical Special Education Accommodations by Sue Watson

http://specialed.about.com/od/iep/a/accomod.htm

National Association of Parents with Children in Special Education: Membership for one to two years required.

www.napcse.org/exceptionalchildren/autism-accommodations-modifications.php

National Dissemination Center for Children with Disabilities

www.nichcy.org

The National Center on Educational Outcomes (NCEO)

www.education.umn.edu/nceo/TopicAreurs

Peer Assisted Learning Strategies

http://kc.vanderbilt.edu/kennedy/pals/

CHAPTER 5
R.E.A.**D**.Y.
DETERMINING LEVELS OF SUPPORT

Assessing for the Appropriate Level of Staff Support

When an IEP team prepares for inclusive education, level of support is an accommodation that must be considered. There are many types of support that may be provided to accommodate a student with ASD or other disabilities. Frequently however, the big question for an IEP team to answer is; does a level of support accommodation automatically equal a paraprofessional assigned to work individually with only one student? This is often called 1:1 support.

In 1996, Pickett reported that there were 280,000 paraprofessionals working in special education settings. Para-professionals were hired to fill many roles including 1:1 support for students in inclusive education. As Paula Kluth (2003), notes many paraprofessional's roles and responsibilities are not clearly defined. It might also be added that frequently, when a 1:1 paraprofessional is assigned, the decision is based on perceived needs not assessed needs.

Decisions based on assessed needs provide the information to carefully craft the role and responsibilities of the paraprofessional providing the accommodation of additional support in inclusive education. The following forms have been developed to provide the IEP team with tools that may assist them in identifying the specific level of needs across three basic areas of concern behavior, instruction, and inclusion. These three areas are especially important when addressing the issues facing students with ASD. The steps to assess for student needs include the following:

1. Assess across all areas of need using a rubric.
2. Evaluate supports that already exist.
3. Determine how much and the type of additional support that is currently required.

Step 1: The first step in the assessment is to complete the *Student Needs Rubric* form. This form is used to identify the generic level of support required across a student's behavior, instruction, and inclusive education setting (See Figure 5.1). The educator or IEP team highlights the boxes that generically identify the level of support that a student currently requires. The *Student Needs Rubric* provides the educator or IEP team with a visual picture of students needs across the identified areas.

The *Student Needs Rubric* may also be scored numerically as shown across the bottom of the form in Figure 5.1. The following example will demonstrate the procedure. The total number from each area is recorded in the spaces provided at the bottom of the page. If the student scored a two in the *Behavior* column, a four in under *Instruction*, and a three best described his *Inclusion*, then when the numbers are added together the total would be nine.

STUDENT NEEDS RUBRIC

Student:	DOB:	Disability:	Date Reviewed:
Current Program:		Educator:	
Review Team Members:			

	Behavior	Instruction	Inclusion
0	Regularly follows adult directions without frequent prompts or close supervision. Handles change and redirection with little stress. Usually gets along with peers and adults. Seeks social interactions but may be awkward.	Can participate fully in whole class instruction. Can stay on task during typical instructional activity. Follows direction with few to no additional prompts.	Participate in most core curriculum within gen. ed. class. Requires few accommodations. Transitions with or without visual supports. Usually tries to socialize with peers, but may be awkward at times.
1	Usually follow adult direction but occasionally requires additional clarification, encouragement and prompts to follow directions. May have occasional difficulty with peers and/or adults. Does not always seek out friends but usually plays if invited.	Participates in group at instructional level but may require additional prompts, cue or reinforcement. Requires reminders to stay on task, follow directions and to remain engaged in learning.	Participates with accommodation and occasional modification. May need occasional visual reminders of schedule changes. Requires some additional support to finish work and be responsible. Needs some social cueing to interact with peers appropriately.
2	Consistently has problems following directions and behaving appropriately. Can be managed adequately with a classroom behavior management plan, accommodations and/or modifications, but would be unable to experience much success without the plan implementation.	Cannot always participate in whole class instruction. May require smaller groups, visual clarification, frequent prompts, cues and reinforcement. On task about 50% of the time with support. May require accommodations to successfully participate in learning.	Participates with visual supervision and occasional prompts. May require visual shadowing to get to class. Regularly needs modifications and accommodations to benefit from class activities. Socialization may require adult facilitation.
3	Has moderate behavior problems almost daily and is likely to be non compliant, defiant and verbally explosive. Requires a Behavior Support Plan (BSP) and behavior goals and objectives on the IEP. Is likely to require close visual supervision to implement BSP.	Difficult to participate in a large group. Requires low student staff ratio, close adult proximity and prompts including physical assistance to stay on task. Primarily complies only with 1:1 directions & monitoring. Cognitive abilities & skills likely require modifications not typical for class as a whole.	Participation may require additional staff for direct instructional and behavioral support. Likely requires direct supervision going to and from class. Always requires modifications and accommodations for class work. Requires adult to facilitate social interaction with peers.
4	Has a serious problem behavior with potential for injury to self and others. Meets Hughes Bill criteria. Functional Analysis Assessment of behavior has been completed and the student has a well developed PBIP which must be implemented to allow the student to safely attend school. A BICM is assigned and staff has been trained in the management of assaultive behavior.	Cannot participate in a group without constant 1:1 support. Requires constant cuing and physical prompting to stay on task and follow directions. Regularly requires specific 1:1 instructional strategies to benefit from the individualized educational program. Cognitive abilities and skills require significant accommodation and modification not typical for the class group.	Always requires 1:1 staff in close proximity for issues such as safety. Direct instruction, mobility or behavior monitoring. Requires 1:1 assistance to go to and from class. Requires adult to facilitate social interaction with peers and remain in close proximity at all times.

Select the number that best describes the student in each rubric category. If a student appears to fall between

descriptive categories a (. 5) may be added to any whole number.

Total number from each area   (B) _____ + (I) _____ + (Inc) _____ = Total Number _____

Total may be divided by 3 to determine the average score.   Summary Comments:

Figure 5.1

On the form the scores would be recorded in this way: (B) 3 + (I) 4 + (Inc) 3 = Total Number 9. The total is then divided by 3, or the number of columns being evaluated, to determine the average score, which in this example is an average score of three. A score of three of four demonstrates a significant need for additional staff support for most to all of the school day. As mentioned on the form the educator or team may find that a student meets some but not all the descriptors at other levels. The evaluator may use a point five (.5) on any of the numbers in the left hand column to clarify the students levels.

The second numerical scoring procedure an educator or team could use to determine the amount of support a student might need is to calculate a percentage of points scored. This can be easily done by using the highest points possible one could score on the rubric, which is twelve, and dividing the student's total score by twelve. Using the example above, if the total number scored is 9 which is divided by 12, the percentage is 75%. Thus, it could be hypothesized that the student might benefit from additional staff support approximately 75% of the time. See Figure 5.2 for a chart that provides the percentages for each score possible. The reader is reminded that this is a non-standardized procedure that gives educators or an IEP team a visual and numerical basis for decision making that provides more substance than a perceived need. The rubric may be used as a stand alone form or as the beginning step in a protocol to systematically look at student needs. The *Student Needs Rubric* is found in the CD at the end of the manual.

Score	% of Support	Score	% of Support	Score	% of Support	Score	% of Support
12	100%	9	75%	6	50%	3	25%
11	92%	8	67%	5	42%	2	17%
10	83%	7	58%	4	33%	1	8%

Figure 5.2 Chart of percentages for each possible whole number score.

Step 2: If the team wishes to look more closely at the specific student needs Step 2 in the protocol may be completed. This step requires the educator to make a more formal request for additional staff support by completing the *Referral for Supplementary Staff Support* form (See Figure 5.3). This form is divided into four parts that assist the educator and team to more closely evaluate the student's needs and the supports that already exist, by asking the following questions:

1. What are the specific areas of intensive need that require additional support?

2. Is there an IEP goal written to address the specific area of need?

3. What are the current interventions and methods of support being used?

4. What does the data document are successful existing supports?

5. What is the current student/staff ratio and entire classroom needs?

REFERRAL FOR SUPPLEMENTARY STAFF SUPPORT

Student:	District:	DOB:
Age: M ☐ F ☐	Grade:	School:
Parent/Guardian		Home Phone:
Address:		Work Phone:

PART 1: Check the areas of intensive need that might indicate additional staff support.

Behavior	Instruction	Inclusion
☐ Behavior Support Plan	☐ Physical Assistance	☐ Direct Instruction
☐ Positive Behavior	☐ Constant Prompting	☐ Physical Support
Intervention Plan	☐ Applied Behavior Analysis	☐ Safety
☐ In Place;	☐ Discrete Trial Training	☐ Close Visual Supervision
☐ In Process	☐ TEACCH	☐ Environmental Supports
☐ Aggressive	☐ Assistive Technology	☐ Organizational Supports
☐ Assaultive	☐ PECS	☐ Accommodations Needed
☐ Self Injurious Behavior	☐ Accommodations Needed	☐ Modifications Needed
☐ Non-Compliant	☐ Modifications Needed	☐ Social Support
☐ Over Active	☐ Other: list	☐ Other: list
☐ Runs Away		
☐ Other: list		

PART 2: Describe EACH area of intensive need marked above and indicate if there is an IEP goal/objective written to address the area. Use additional paper if needed to describe all the needs.

PART 3: Describe interventions used to support referred student in EACH of the areas of marked above. Provide data that documents the success or failure of interventions.

PART 4: Describe current classroom staff and student needs: Student/Staff ratio: _____
Number of students requiring assistance in: Behavior: _____ Instruction: _____ Inclusion: _____

Other specific general classroom needs:

This referral is made at the request of ☐ Educator ☐ Parent/Guardian ☐
Other_____
Referring Person_____ Date: _____
Program Administrator Signature **Required:** _____ Date: _____

Figure 5.3

Part 1 lists possible reasons that would prompt a staff to request additional support for a student. These are not all inclusive lists. If there are additional reasons for support these reasons should also be listed. Two other areas, which were not included on this form; however do prompt the need for additional support are health and personal care issues. A rubric and referral form that address these two areas of need, as well as the three areas seen on Figure 5.3 may be found on the CD of forms at the back of this manual.

Part 2 and 3 require the educator to carefully review the contents of the IEP. The educator completing the *Referral for Supplementary Staff Support* form may either write a description in the space provided or use the *PART 2 & 3: Analysis of IEP Goals Form* (See Figure 5.4) which is provided in the CD in the back of this manual. This form allows the educator to provide the information

REFERRAL FOR SUPPLEMENTARY STAFF SUPPORT
PART 2 & 3: Analysis of IEP Goals Form

Area for Additional Support			IEP Goals	Data Progress Documentation		
Behavior	Instruction	Inclusion	Briefly write a description of the goals that have been written to address the areas that require additional support. Check (✓) the area in the columns to the left. Check (✓) the data that best describes progress to the right. Provide quantifiable information that supports data in description space below.	Excellent	OK, but slow	Limited

Figure 5.4

143

requested in Part 2 and 3 on a one page from. If the *Analysis of IEP Goals Form* is used, the form may be attached to the referral page.

Part 4 requests that the educator provide an overview of the expectations for all students in the classroom. Since the *Referral for Supplementary Staff Support* form may be used in both a general education setting and a specialized educational setting to determine the need for additional staff support, the information provided in Part 4 is very important. There may be only one or several students in the general education setting that require varying degrees of additional support. Whereas, in a specialized learning environment, such as a special day class, resource room, or learning center, typically the entire student population requires some degree of additional support. If the referral is being made for a student who is being served in a special day class, the educator or team may decide to complete the *Student Needs Rubric* on each student to determine the overall support needs for the class as a whole. This information can then be reported in Part 4.

Since the *Referral for Supplementary Staff Support* form shown in Figure 5.3 may be considered as a formal referral request for additional individual support, typically an administrator's signature is required. The administrator's signature ensures that all the formal IEP members are in the "communication loop" regarding the concerns of the parents and/or educators. Once again the reader is reminded that this is not a standardized tool, therefore the requirements that are suggested should be considered as guidelines for those choosing to use this protocol.

Step 3: The team may choose to use this step to determine how much and the type of additional support that is currently required. This step is accomplished with a structured observation by an impartial professional who has knowledge and expertise in the identified disability, as well as appropriate interventions and classroom structure.

The protocol for the completion of this step is as follows:

1. The educator completes columns 1 through 4 on the *Current Staff Support Schedule* (See Figure 5.5).

2. An impartial knowledgeable professional is invited to observe the classroom program using the *Current Staff Support Schedule* provided by the educator.

3. The observer records comments and suggestions in column 5 on the *Current Staff Support Schedule*.

4. A team meeting is held to discuss the observational results and determine a plan to support the student including additional adult support if found to be needed.

CURRENT STAFF SUPPORT SCHEDULE

Student: _____ Grade: _____ Teacher: _____

Observer _____ Observation Date(s): _____

Complete for the entire day. Use additional forms as needed.

1. Time/Schedule: List duration and general schedule of activities per day.	2. Group Size: Number students in group per period.	3. IEP Goals/Objectives: Identify briefly the referred student's instructional focus and IEP goal during each period of the day. Highlight goals that relate to the referral for aide support.	4. Description of Staff Support:: What is staff doing now to support referred student each period. Be specific	5. Observation by Outside Observer: Be specific in describing activities and support and potentially required in the classroom for the referred student.

Figure 5.5

Step 3 does not need to be completed unless the team or administrator determines that more data is required before the determination of what the student's exact needs for support are. The impartial professional's observational data will provide the team with information about the day that may have not been considered. The impartial perspective often reveals ideas for support that the staff had not thought of before. Suggestions for staff coverage, structure, additional or different accommodations and modifications that might be of assistance are offered for consideration. This information will give the team a very clear picture of when support is needed and what level of support is required. The impartial professional observer does not make the decision to add additional staff support, their role is to reference to times during the day when the additional support may be necessary for the student to meet educational goals and receive educational benefit.

The ultimate decision to provide additional staff support for a student with ASD or any other disability, will be determined by the IEP team. The three steps and accompanying forms were developed to assist the IEP team make this critical decision with informal assessment data. These forms have been used to informally assess student's needs with a positive outcome for all. Each step of this protocol may be completed as a stand alone procedure or all three steps of this protocol may be completed. The latter provides the IEP team with informal, but comprehensive assessment data which gives an in-depth picture of the student's needs for additional support and the times of the day the additional support would be most helpful.

Determining the Purpose of Staff Support

Besides the individually identified areas of need identified in Part 1 of the *Referral for Supplementary Staff Support*, it must be acknowledged that there are multifaceted purposes of support regardless of the provider which may include any or all of the following:

- Minimize anxiety and discomfort
- Increase stability
- Promote understanding
- Aid information processing
- Provide cues for performance
- Exert positive influence of behavior
- Shore up the functioning abilities
- Enhance overall student learning
- Enhance social, play and leisure skill development
- Promote independence and competence

When the purpose of the support is clearly identified the team may choose to detail the type of support provided in the inclusive environment. It may be helpful to establish this support in a written format. Several forms have been developed which will assist all implementers in clearly understanding their role and the expectations for the focus student within a classroom (See Figures 5.6 and 5.7).

It has been noted by many that too often paraprofessional are asked to design curriculum or instruction, conduct formal and informal assessments, create adaptations for students, and make a range of other critical instructional decision on their own (Downing, Ryndak, & Clark, 2000; Giangreco, Broer, & Edelman, 1999; Marks, Schrader, & Levine, 1999). Many of these requests are over and above expectations an educator should have for a paraprofessional. This situation typically stems from the difficulty staff experiences finding adequate collaboration time to review expectations with the paraprofessionals or other additional staff. The *Staff Responsibilities Plan* (See Figure 5.6) and the *Classroom Participation Plan* (See Figure 5.7) forms were developed to address the lack of collaboration time that educators frequently experience. These forms create a written plan for staff to follow which outlines the student and staff expectations. These forms are included on the CD at the back of this manual.

The *Staff Responsibility Plan* (See Figure 5.6) gives the teacher a simple, easy to follow form which clearly identifies what the staff and student expectations are for every period of the day.

STAFF RESPONSIBILITIES PLAN

Student: _Joe_ Staff: _Paraprofessional_ Teacher: _Bishop_

Student's Schedule/ Activity	Direct Instructional Support and Student Goals	Visual Support and Structure	Organizational Support Set Up/Clean Up
Calendar	Sit facing teacher, place numbers in correct order, point to correct day and month	--individual calendar with numbers --pages with days of the week and months	Have a choice of three numbers ready for them to choose from
Reading center	Stay at table with group, match identical letters, imitate letter sounds	--letter cards and fidgets box while waiting for a turn	Have student retrieve task box for reading group

Figure 5.6 Sample of a plan for second grade

The *Staff Responsibility Plan* (See Figure 5.6) form provides a method to concretely explain to the paraprofessional three very important pieces of information to successfully work with the focus student every period of the day. The educator first fills in column one with the student's daily *Schedule/Activities*. Next, the educator identifies *Direct Instructional Support and Student Goals* in column two, *Visual Support* and *Structure* in column three, and column four will identify the *Organizational Support Set Up/Clean Up*. This simple form may be used at any grade level to provide staff with a very clear picture "at-one-glance" of student and staff expectations, even when there has not been time for verbal collaboration and clarification.

In some inclusive situations there may be the need to have a more detailed plan that explains the level of student participation expected by the focus student. To meet this need the *Classroom Participation Plan* form was developed. (See Figure 5.7) It is recommended that the special and general educator complete this form together, to ensure that both educators share the same expectation for the student and the paraprofessional who will be working in the inclusive setting. The educators must identify the class activity and what all the typical students are expected to be doing. Next they briefly describe how the focus student will participate and his or her targeted skills or goals for instruction. The educators then identify the accommodations, modifications, materials, equipment etc. that they will provide for the class activity. Once the paraprofessional is familiar with these additional supports, it may be expected the paraprofessional sets them up for the student. Any additional supports should be listed in the last section of the plan.

Educators may choose to write a detailed *Classroom Participation Plan* for every period of the day or just specific period that requires more detailed information to clarify expectations and support. This plan is more similar to a specific lesson plan than just an overview of expectations. The details of the plan are typically reviewed at progress reporting times or when other significant changes might be occurring in the student's schedule. Thus, once educators have written these plans they can be used for several weeks or months, depending on the situation. Educators have found the *Classroom Participation Plan* to be extremely helpful when either a substitute teacher or paraprofessional is needed. Educators have reported that because the *Classroom Participation Plan* was available potentially difficult situations were avoided.

The final tool that is helpful in defining opportunities for instruction is called a "R.E.A.D.Y Matrix". The structure of the matrix gives an educator a very simple format to show the relationship between the periods or activities of the day and an individual student's instructional goals. The R.E.A.D.Y. Matrix format has been used to identify other opportunities during the day where social and friendship skills, communication skill, and other skill categories might be addressed or directly instructed throughout the day.

CLASSROOM PARTICIPATION PLAN

Student: Joe	Grade & Educator: 2nd Miss Sunshine	Date Developed: 9/15/08
Class Activity: Reading Workbooks		

Description of Class Activity:
- Students take their workbooks out of their desks with a pencil.
- They look to the board to check which pages are assigned.
- Each student works independently.
- Students raise their hand if they need help.
- When they finish the assigned pages they place their workbook in a stack on the reading table.
- If they finish early they may read their library book

How student will participate in this class activity:
- Joe will get his pencil off the side of his stacking trays
- Joe's reading pages have been separated and placed in folders in the top of stacking trays on his desk
- A picture of his self selected reinforcer is place on the top of his visual timer and the timer is set for 15 minutes
- As he finishes each folder he places it in the bottom tray
- If he finishes at or before 15 minutes he earns his reward and then may read his library book

Targeted Skills/Goal for Instruction:
1. Completing activity at the appropriate rate
2. Following a routine

Accommodations, Modifications, Materials, Equipment Etc. Needed:
Work is separated, a work system is used, his pencil is stuck to the tray with Velcro, a Time Timer is used with a selected visual reinforcer for a quick or timely finish

Person(s) responsible: 2nd grade educator and special educator

Other Supports:
Peers may assist Joe if he gets off track by pointing out what section he should be working on. While the work system is being taught to Joe close adult supervision may be needed and more frequent reinforcement. Initially Joe may complete one folder and then move to 2 or more as he becomes proficient with the system.

Figure 5.7 Sample of second grade student's plan

The matrix format was introduced in the *Individual Critical Skills Model* (Holowach 1998) to assist teachers who were working with students with moderate to severe disabilities identify when their student's goals could be addressed within the classroom schedule or in an inclusive setting. The format was presented again in *Curriculum Adaptations for Inclusive Classrooms,* by the PEERS Project 1992. The sample seen in Figure 5.8 demonstrates how the *R.E.A.D.Y Matrix for Measurable Annual Goals and Daily Schedule* could be used to identify times during the day when specific instruction might occur. The *R.E.A.D.Y. Matrix* gives educators and an IEP team a clear visual idea "at-one-glance" times when specific instruction could occur. This form may be used as a stand alone form for the experienced educator or paraprofessional. It may also be used as the first step in completing the *Staff Responsibilities Plan* (See Figure 5.6) and the *Classroom Participation Plan* (See Figure 5.7) forms discussed previously. The matrix format has been expanded by other authors (Halvorsen and Neary, 2001) to provide even more information that would be helpful to staff by looking at selected school subjects and activities.

INFUSION MATRIX FOR MEASURABLE ANNUAL GOALS AND CLASSROOM SCHEDULE

Directions: Insert a ✔ when there is an opportunity to work on a student's goal within the daily schedule. Use the information gathered on this form to develop instructional plans using the *Staff Responsibility Plan* form or *Classroom Participate Plan* form.

Classroom Schedule

IEP Goals	Turn in homework	Flag Salute	Journal Write	Reading Workbook	Reading Lg. Group	Social Studies	RECESS	Accelerated Math	Saxon Math	LUNCH	Music	Art	PE
Follows group instructions					✓	✓			✓		✓	✓	✓
Completes activities at an appropriate rate			✓	✓	✓	✓		✓	✓				
Follows (imitates) gross motor movements		✓					✓			✓			✓
Follows general routines	✓	✓	✓				✓			✓			✓
Takes turns in activities with peers							✓			✓			✓
Responds to the conversations of peers							✓			✓			
Writes a sentence w/ punctuation			✓			✓							
Identifies math function, completes problems								✓	✓				
Answers "wh" questions			✓	✓	✓	✓	✓	✓	✓	✓	✓	✓	✓

Figure 5.8 Sample R.E.A.D.Y. Matrix for Elementary age

Although the *R.E.A.D.Y. Matrix* form may be used successfully with any grade student from kindergarten to twelfth grade, a
variation of the format has been created for the middle school and
high school age student. (See Figure 5.9) This format includes
criteria for mastery along with the scheduled opportunities for instruction. Educators have found that the matrix format has been
a very helpful method to convey a large amount of information on
one page. It also provides a very simple procedure for integrating
a variety of skills across the day.

IEP INFUSION MATRIX
MIDDLE SCHOOL AND HIGH SCHOOL SCHEDULE

Goals for: _____ Week Of: _____ Staff: _____

Shaded areas represent times where goals should be worked on and data will be recorded.
In box, indicate date and criteria level achieved on that date. Goals should be worked on daily during the designated times,
data should be collected on each goal during the designated periods at least 1 x per week.

	Goal 1: Comply w/in 15 sec. of 2nd request.	Goal 2: On task for 10, 20, 30 min.	Goal 3: Write assign. In log w/prompt	Goal 4: Write paragraph of 5 sentences	Goal 5: Complete assign. in log by record date	Goal 6: Math: Add & Sub	Goal 7: Emergency words	Goal 8: Reading Comp. How & Why ?s
1st Period Lang Arts								
2nd Period I. Science								
3rd Period US History								
4th Period F. Math								
5th Period Lunch								
6th Period Vet Science								
7th Period Vet Science								
Criteria per Goal listed in first row →	75 – 100 % 50 – 74 % 25 – 49% > 25%	30 min 20 min 10 min > 10 min	4-5 prompts 3-4 prompts 1-2 prompts Refused	Submit weekly samples to Teacher for portfolio	Submit daily SOP to Teacher for portfolio	80–100 % 60 – 79 % 40 – 59% 20 – 39% Refused	MET	10:10 8:10 6:10 4:10 >3:10
Goal Status for the week								

Figure 5.9

In summary, there are a variety of supports that may be implemented to assist a student with ASD or other disabilities in an inclusive setting. If additional staff support is a consideration there should be some protocol in place to determine the need. After a systematic assessment, if an IEP team determines that additional staff support is required then it is critical that the staff be given training and written plans which outline the methods for implementing the support. The *Staff Responsibility Plan, Classroom Participation Plan*, and *R.E.A.D.Y. Matrix* offer educators a few simple tools to assist the paraprofessional or others who are providing additional support.

REFERENCES

Downing, J., Ryndak, D., & Clark, D. Para-educators in inclusive classrooms: Their own perspective. *Remedial and Special Education, 21*, 171-181. 2000.

Giangreco, M. E., Broer, S. M., & Edelman, S. W., The tip of the iceberg: Determining whether paraprofessional support is needed for students with disabilities in general education settings. *The Journal of the Association for Persons with Severe Handicaps*, 24, 280-290, 1999.

Holowach, K.T. *Teaching the works: The individualized critical skills model*. Sacramento, CA. California Department of Education, 1989.

Halvorsen, A. and Neary, T. *Building Inclusive Schools: Tools and Strategies for Success*. Needham Heights, MA: Allyn and Bacon, 2001.

Kluth, Paula. *"You're Going to Love This Kid!" Teaching Students with Autism in the Inclusive Classroom.* Baltimore: Paul H. Brookes Publishing Co, 2003.

Neary, T., Halvorsen, A., Kronberg, R. and Kelly, D. *Curriculum Adaptations for Inclusive Classrooms*. San Francisco, CA: California Research Institute on the Integration of Students with Severe Disabilities, 1992.

Pickett, A. A State of the Art Reports on Para-educators in Education and Related Services. National Resource Center for Para-professionals in Education and Related Services, Center for Advanced Study in Education. New York, NY: The Graduate School and University Center, City University of New York, 1996.

RESOURCES

Ashbaker, B. Y. and Morgan, J. *Paraprofessionals in the Classroom.* USA: Allyn and Bacon, 2005.

Ashbaker, B. Y. and Morgan, J. A *Teacher's Guide to Working with Paraeducators and Other Classroom Aides.* Alexandria, VA: Association for Supervision and Development, 2001.

Doyle, M. B. *The Paraprofessional's Guide to the Inclusive Classroom: Working as a Team.* Baltimore MD: Paul H. Brookes Publishing Co. 2002.

Hammeken, P. A. *Inclusion: An Essential Guide for the Paraprofessional – A Practical Reference Tool for All Paraprofessional Working in Inclusive Settings.* Minnetonka, MN: Peytral Publications, 2003

Marks, S. U., Schrader, C., & Levine, M. Para-educator experiences in inclusive settings: Helping, hovering or holding their own? *Exceptional Children*, 65, 315-328, 1999.

National Research Council. *Educating Children with Autism.* Washington DC: National Academy Press, 2001.

Twachtman-Cullen, D. *How to be a Para Pro: A Comprehensive Training Manual for Paraprofessionals.* Higganum, CT: Starfish Specialty Press, 2000.

Twachtman-Cullen, D. and Twachtman-Reilly, J. *How Well Does Your IEP Measure Up?* Higganum, CT: Starfish Specialty Press, 2002.

CHAPTER 6

R.E.A.D.**Y.**
Your Natural Supports: Peers

Activities to Build Autism Awareness and Develop Friendships

The number of children identified with an Autism Spectrum Disorder (ASD) has dramatically increased at an alarming rate over the last decade. As the number of students with ASD continues to increase, the public schools have seen more students with these unique needs enter their classrooms. The level of support required to meet the needs of students with ASD is typically addressed through the IEP process. Even with a well developed IEP, professionals may still feel overwhelmed when trying to meet the student's need consistently throughout the day. This is especially true in the area of social interaction.

The professional's concern is valid because social demands happen everywhere there are people and students with ASD need some degree of support to handle these ever changing social demands. By turning to the research professionals will discover a solution to their dilemma. The research reveals that there is a large body of human recourses that is accessible at every school and can provide consistent daily support, especially in the area of socializations. Thus, we find the solution to our dilemma in this largely untapped human resource, the typical peer group. These human resources can be utilized with any age of students from preschool through college. Ozonoff, Rogers, and Hendren (2003) report that peer mediated intervention for improving social behavior has produced the largest body of published work. The research has shown that untrained but motivated typical peers may make a difference in the life of a student with ASD or other disability. The studies also reveal that when the typical peer has had some awareness training the outcomes for the student with disabilities can be even greater.

The National Research Council noted in *Educating Children with Autism* (2001) that, "In the peer-mediated approach, developed over the past 20 years by Phillip Strain, Samuel Odem, Howard Goldstein, and their associates, typical peers are taught to repeatedly initiate 'play organizers' such as sharing, helping, giving affection, and praise." Other studies (Hoyson et al., 1984; Strain et al., 1979; Strain et al., 1977; Goldstein et al., 1992) noted the power of these peer mediated strategies to increase not only social interaction, but maintenance and generalization of the social skills at the preschool level. Oke and Schreibman (1990) and McGee and colleagues (1992) expanded upon past studies and found similar positive results when typical peers where trained to promote appropriate social interaction in children with autism. These approaches have been assembled by Danko et al., 1998 into a chapter and have also been described in other publications.

An additional point of interest revealed in the research is that "interactions established between children with autism and adults do not easily generalize to peer partners" (Bartak and Rutter, 1973). Given this information, it is important to take an intentional step in a general education classroom to, at the very least, begin a foundation for the development of a relationship between the typical peers and the students with an Autism Spectrum Disorder or other disability, which is built on a shared understanding.

The purpose of this chapter is to meet the needs of professionals to provide trained human resources to students with ASD by providing a structured procedure that can help both parents and professionals begin the learning and awareness process for typical peers. Historically similar activities were called "Disability Awareness". The activities might focus on one specific disability group or on several types of disabilities. Some of the activities involved puppets, video or simulation activities. These activities create a general awareness of diversity, but often do not share information that could provide a foundation for a friendship and individual support.

This chapter differs from disability awareness because it begins by focusing on abilities and friendships, not the disability. To move to the level of friendship, information needs to be shared in a different way. Friendship is based on a shared history, likes, dislikes and proximity. Friendships typically last over a period of time and are characterized by a preference to be together while engaging in reciprocal, helpful, and positive interactions.

Unfortunately, when a student with a disability enters a general education classroom many of the characteristics of a friendship are typically missing. Oftentimes, there is not a shared history because students with ASD may not start at the beginning of the year; or they may not be attending their neighborhood school. This requires the teachers, school staff, and parents to come together to develop a plan that will foster friendships.

This chapter provides a simple planning form to gather basic information for the activity. The basic steps for implementing the awareness activity are described. Variations on the ability awareness theme are presented to provide ideas for various age groups, as well as, ideas for introducing information about the student's disability. Case studies give the reader real life examples of how the activities have proven to develop support and friendship for a student with ASD. This chapter also offers the reader an extensive list of resources including books for every age group, along with books to assist the student with ASD in developing a self awareness.

This chapter may be used as a guideline or a facilitator may follow the steps as they are specifically outlined. The reader is reminded that ability awareness is not a once a year activity. The resources provide additional ideas for on-going understanding of ASD and relationships. The ultimate goal is that by using this chapter parents and professional will develop a plan that will lead to a support network of peers, which the research indicates promotes better opportunities for social success for the student with an Autism Spectrum Disorder or other disability.

SECTION 1: GETTING STARTED

What Makes School Great? FRIENDS! is an awareness activity designed to develop a shared knowledge of common interests and a foundation for friendship, understanding, and support for a peer with an Autism Spectrum Disorder (ASD) or other disability. The activity may be facilitated by any school staff member (general or special educator, speech pathologist, school psychologist, program specialist, administrator, or para-educator) who feels comfortable leading a group of students through the steps.

To implement an awareness activity the facilitator will need to do some planning and preparation. The following *PLANNING CHECKLIST* (See Table 6.1) provides the facilitator a tool to gather information that is necessary to implement an ability awareness activity.

What Makes School Great? FRIENDS!
PLANNING CHECKLIST

Section 1: Basic Information

Student	Grade	School
Date of Activity	Time	Length
Parent	Phone	
Parent Permission Granted: YES ☐; NO ☐	Date	By
Teacher	Phone	
Other		

Section 2: Purpose and Participation

Expected Outcome:	Comment:
General Knowledge: ☐ Specific Knowledge: ☐ Other: ☐	Describe
Parent Participation: YES ☐; NO ☐ If YES, How? Attend: ☐ Other: ☐	Describe:
Student Participation: No ☐; Yes ☐ If yes, How? Attend: ☐ Other: ☐	Describe:

Section 3: Student Information for Shared Understanding

Likes and Interests	Strengths	Things that are hard

Figure 6.1

The checklist is divided into 3 sections which cover Basic Information (See Figure 6.2), Purpose and Participation (See Figure 6.3), and Student Information for Shared Understanding (See Figure 6.4). The following instructions will assist the facilitator complete each section of the *PLANNING CHECKLIST.*

Section 1: Basic Information

Student		Grade	School
Date of Activity		Time	Length
Parent		Phone	
Parent Permission Granted: YES ☐; NO ☐		Date	By
Teacher		Phone	
Other			

Figure 6.2

Form 1: Basic Information

This section provides a place to keep all pertinent basic information regarding the activity. The grade level of the class is very important information as it will help determine the type of presentation and the length of time that will be spent with the group. The younger the age group, the shorter the length of the presentation. Some schools may request that several classes at a specific grade level be included in a single presentation or they may want to provide the information for all primary or intermediate classes. Large group awareness activities can be successfully presented; however when the goal is to develop personal relationships more student participation is required which is difficult in a very large group. To facilitate more personal interaction and begin to build shared knowledge it is recommended that no more than two classes come together for an activity. If time permits, it is always preferable to address one classroom at a time.

It is important to have the contact information for the parent and the classroom teacher, or lead teacher if several classes will be addressed at one time. Parents should be aware of any type of awareness activities because whether the activity is on a general topic such as friendship or a disability specific topic, it will have a direct impact on their child's skills within the classroom. This is especially true for students with ASD who have a core deficit in the area of socialization and relationships. If it is a disability specific activity, even if the child is not going to be singled out, the parent should be informed and requested to give permission to proceed with the activity.

The very youngest student recognizes differences in others. By doing a disability specific activity a facilitator may inadvertently draw attention to the student with the disability, thus starting questions that possibly neither the professional nor parent are ready to respond to. The request for permission is also an invitation for participation.

Section 2: Purpose and Participation

Expected Outcome:	Comment:
General Knowledge: ☐ Specific Knowledge: ☐ Other: ☐	Describe
Parent Participation: YES ☐; NO ☐ If YES, How? Attend: ☐ Other: ☐	Describe:
Student Participation: YES ☐; NO ☐ If YES, How? Attend: ☐ Other: ☐	Describe:

Figure 6.3

Form 2: Purpose and Participation

The expected outcome and type of participation by the parent and student with ASD or other disability may be simply outlined in this section. There should always be a discussion to determine the general purpose and expected outcome of the activity with the general educator and parent either together or separately. As mentioned before, an awareness activity is more than just a one-time event. Ability awareness must become an on-going growth process that begins with one event.

General Knowledge: The *General Knowledge* box should be checked if the activity is to present any general information such as friendship, similarities and differences, teasing, bullying, or meeting someone new. The box to the right may be used to briefly describe the desired outcome.

Specific Knowledge: The *Specific Knowledge* box should be checked when either a specific disability or disabilities are going to be presented. This box should also be checked if a specific child is going to be discussed whether or not his/her disability will be discussed. If the specific disability is going to be discussed it is extremely important for the facilitator to know, prior to the activity, the degree to which the specific child understands his/her own disability. Depending on the level of understanding and age of the student it might be important to get his/her permission as well. The right to confidentiality prevails in all specific awareness activities. Thus, even if it appears that it would be helpful for peers to understand why a student with a disability relates to others in a different way, it is imperative that if parents and/or student do not want to share personal information that their wishes are respected. When a family is hesitant to share personal information the facilitator should only provide a general awareness activity. The space on the right can be used to note comments on participation.

Parent Participation: Parents of the focus student should always have the option of attending and participating in the awareness activities whether the activity is general or specific in nature. Depending on the type of the activity, some parents may want to attend as an observer to gain the knowledge of what their child and the classmates are learning. Other parents may only feel comfortable verbally providing background information needed in Section 3 (See Figure 6.4), prior to the specific activity. There have been parents who have created photo collages and small story books about their child to be shared with classmates. Occasionally, parents have volunteered to bring a special treat for the class after the activity. Parents who feel comfortable speaking in the class may choose to participate as a contributor from the audience or as the leader of an activity to share things like family history, dreams, likes, strengths, dislikes and areas in which their child may require help. Regardless of the level of parent participation, collaboration with parent of the focus student is vital to the success of awareness activities. Parent participation has been observed to have a powerful impact on both student and professional participants. It is a very visual and concrete way to show general education students that the student with disabilities is more like them than they are different. Meeting the parent of any classmate contributes to a shared history and understanding.

Student Participation: The decision to include the student with disabilities in either a general or specific awareness activity is dependent on several variables. The first variable is the preference of the parents. Parents know their child and should make this decision. Professionals may share their opinions as to the pros and cons of a student's participation, but the final decision should be the parents.

A few reasons to include the student with disabilities in an awareness activity include but are not limited to the following:

- The activity is general and may help the student learn foundational friendship skills.

- The activities are planned to form peer groups based on interests.

- If the activity is incorporated into a "Student or Star of the Week" the student may enjoy the individual attention.

- The student has requested awareness activities to help his/her peers understand ASD and how friendship may be difficult. These requests have been made by students as young as 1st grade and up through high school. The average age for a student to request this activity is fourth to eight grade.

A few reasons NOT to include the student with disabilities in an awareness activity include, but are not limited to the following:

- The student's attention span and ability to participate would prevent successful participation.

- The student has no awareness of his/her disability and might be confused by a specific discussion.

- There are specific problematic behaviors that need to be addressed which might make both the student with disabilities and other students uncomfortable.

- The student with disabilities does not want to participate.

Section 3: Student Information for Shared Interest

Likes and Interests	Strengths	Things that are hard

Figure 6.4

Form 3: Student Information for Shared Interest

This section (See Figure 6.4), of the *PLANNING CHECKLIST* is provided for the facilitator to gather, prior to the activity, personal information about the student with ASD or other disabilities. This information can be used in either general or student specific awareness activities.

Likes and Interests: Identifying likes and interests is very important because common interests and preferences are part of the foundation for building a friendship. This information can be used in a general friendship building activities without identifying the student by:

- Covertly assisting the student with ASD to join others that have similar interests.
- Using the likes and interests of the student with ASD as the basis for forming activity groups.

This information can be used in specific awareness activities by:

- Listing the likes and interests and asking for a show of hands to indicate who likes the same thing. Next the facilitator may introduce the student with disabilities as a peer who likes all the things listed.
- Using the list to develop related interests.
- Using the list to identify new knowledge about a peer.

Strengths: It is important to recognize that everyone has strengths even if they have a disability. Strengths can be used to develop friendships. A common response that any typical child gives when asked "What a friend might do?" is to say "My friend helps me sometimes."

Information on a student's strengths can be used in a general friendship building activity without identifying the student by:

- Identifying the strength and soliciting ideas about how a person with that strength could be a helpful friend.
- Using the strengths of a student with ASD as the basis for

forming activity groups who could plan how they might help others who don't share the same strength.

This information can be used in specific awareness activities by:
- Asking the student to identify his/her strength (what he/she is good at) and what these strengths help him/her do.
- Having typical peers identify what the student with ASD is good at and share how that strength could help them.

Things That Are Hard: Although oftentimes the things that are hard for the student with ASD are the reasons that an awareness activity is planned, the difficulties should not be the whole focus of any awareness activity. Every person has things that are more difficult for them. Recognizing that everyone needs help on the things that are difficult is part of awareness activities and friendship. As the children always say, "My friends help me."   It is learning to give and receive the help that may be the challenge for the student with disabilities, as well as other students.

Information about what is hard for a student can be used in a general friendship building activities without identifying the student by:
- Covertly identifying what is hard and soliciting ideas about how a friend could help that person.
- Using the things that are hard for the student with ASD as the basis for forming peer support groups who could work together on similar issues.

This information can be used in specific awareness activities by:
- Asking the student to identify things that are hard for him to do and what helps him.

- Having typical peers identify what they think is difficult and how they could be a helpful friend.

A completed sample *PLANNING CHECKLIST* concludes the chapter. (See Figure 6.5) The sample *PLANNING CHECKLIST* has been completed using anonymous names and locations. Any similarity to real persons or locations is purely coincidental.

What Makes School Great?
PLANNING CHECKLIST

Section 1: Basic Information

Student: Fred Jones	Grade: 3rd	School: Ross Elementary
Date of Activity: 09-10-08	Time: 10:15	Length: 45 minutes
Parent: Fay Jones	Phone	
Parent Permission Granted: YES ☑; NO ☐	Date: 09-03-08	By: Program Specialist
Teacher: Mrs. Day	Phone: 000-222-3333	
Other: Mr. Sims, Principal		

Section 2: Purpose and Participation

Expected Outcome:	Comment:
General Knowledge: ☐ Specific Knowledge: ☑ Other: ☐ Fred is new to Ross Elem. Parents want peers to understand him.	Describe: Fred wants to have friends, but he has difficulty making friends due to his lack of social understanding.
Parent Participation: YES ☑; NO ☐ If YES, How? Attend: ☑ Other: ☑	Describe: Mom will bring pictures of Fred's family and a small treat for after the activity.
Student Participation: YES ☑; NO ☐ If YES, How? Attend: ☑ Other: ☑	Describe: Fred knows he has Autism, but it does not bother him. He will answer questions about Section 3 during the activity.

Section 3: Student Information for Shared Interest

Likes and Interests:	Strengths:	Things that are hard:
- Disney movies - Reading - Drawing - Playing the piano	- Good reader - Great Speller - Happy most of the time - Wants to do a good job	- Math - Playing at recess - Knowing the rules - Thinking about other's interests

Figure 6.5

SECTION 2: BASIC STEPS FOR AWARENESS ACTIVITY
What Makes School Great? FRIENDS!

Introducing a Student with Disabilities to a General Education Classroom. The following seven steps are designed to cover the topics of friendship, how to be a friend, and what friends share. This awareness activity may be implemented as presented or with any number of variations based on the expected outcomes as identified on the *PLANNING CHECKLIST* (See Figure 6.1) or the age of the group. This format has been successfully used in classes from kindergarten through high school with the appropriate modifications to make each step appropriate to the age group.

The outcome of this specific "What Makes School Great?" activity is to introduce the student with disabilities (identified in this chapter as the "focus student") to his general education peers. The focus student might be a student who spends all or part of his day in the general education setting. Regardless of the amount of time in spent in the class, the student still requires support building friendships.

Step 1: Identifying Feelings before School Starts. Ask the students to think back to the night before the first day of school and share their feelings. Have the adults in the audience share their feelings too.

Facilitator Options:
- For younger children the facilitator can capture interest by pretending to give everyone a new thinking cap from a magic box. The students may be instructed to adjust

their "thinking cap" or even describe them before asking to recall their feelings.

- A simple face may be drawn on the board to provide a visual reference to the feelings the students name.
- Their feelings may be written on the board.
- Ask for a show of hands to determine how many students shared the same feelings.

Participant Responses:
- These usually range from happy and excited to nervous or scared.
- Students may have more than one emotion to share.

Step 2: Identifying What Makes School Great. Ask the students and staff to share what made them feel great once they got to school on the first day. The purpose of this guided question is to arrive at the conclusion that friends, old or new, are what makes school great. The response that will be the topic starter for Step 3 is FRIENDS.

Facilitator Options:
- Draw a picture to provide a visual reference of comments.
- Write what made them feel great on the board.
- Take a vote or ask for a show of hands to confirm that all agree the number one thing that made school great for them was friends and move on to the next step.

Participant Responses:
- There will be a variety of responses; however, within the first five responses typically a student will comment that

either having friends, or seeing old friends, or making new friends is "What makes school great"!

Step 3: Identifying Elements of Friendship. Ask the students and staff to name one thing they like to do with friends or what being a friend means. Adjust the question to the age of the group. Watch for activities that have been identified by the focus student so they may be integrated into Step 4.

Facilitator Options:
- Draw a picture to provide a visual reference.
- Write their thoughts on the board.
- Take a vote on agreement of each idea as it is shared.
- A vote may be taken to select the top three ideas about what being a friend means.

Participant Responses:
- Young students may name more activities such as play ball, play tag etc. If this is the case then the facilitator might add the concepts of sharing, helping, taking turns and thinking more about their friend than themselves.

Step 4: Identifying Who Shares the Same Interests with the Focus Student. Using the list of the focus student's favorite items ask the class, "Who would like a friend who likes -----?" (List the items that are preferred by the focus student either verbally or visually.)

Facilitators Option:
- Write or draw the focus student's preferences on the board.

173

- The names of the students who share the same preference may be written beside the list of the focus student's preferences, or note when 100% if the entire class shares the preference.

Participants Responses:
- There are usually many hands raised for each item and frequently the entire class shares the preference.
- The participants enthusiasm is typically growing at this point.

Step 5: Introducing the New Student. After it is determined that most of the participants would like a friend who likes all the things that were listed the facilitator announces to them that, "It is your lucky day because there is a student in this class (or grade) that likes all those things too." Then the focus student is introduced. The facilitator may explain how the focus student was a little nervous to come to this new school or class, but now is excited to have classmates who share some of his or her favorite interests.

Facilitators Option:
- If the focus student is present and capable of commenting on his/her interests the facilitator may ask for more details or open it up to the class.
- If the focus student's parent is in the audience they may add additional information.
- If the focus student is not present, but will be joining the class later the peers may be prompted to develop ways to incorporate the new classmate's interest into the day and make school great for everyone.

Participants Responses:
- The participants typically all have a positive attitude about meeting a new person with whom they share interests.
- There will be some participants who will immediately show an interest in pursing a relationship and others who will not. Both responses are appropriate and should be respected. With younger participant a larger number of students want to form a friendship. As children age and strong relationship are developed they may be less likely to add a new person to their friendship group.

Step 6: Develop a Plan for Expanding the Friendship with the New Student. Further explore the shared interest with the students. Following this discussion make a plan for the shared interests to grow within the class, on the playground, or at home. If the student is present then include him/her as appropriate.

Facilitators Option:
- List the student's ideas to strengthen friendship with the new student and other students in the class.
- Develop an action plan to implement the ideas listed.
- Put the action plan in writing as appropriate to the age group.
- Identify students who would like to help. This step may be left as a classroom follow-up assignment.

Participant Responses:
- Acknowledge what is typical for the age group. Based on the type of response this step may be completed with a small group of interested students at a different time

Step 7: Recognize All Participants. Congratulate the students for their wonderful ideas about friendship and their participation in welcoming a new student to their class. End the activity with a small treat. If this treat is provided by the parent then the focus student may choose peers to help distribute the treat.

SECTION 3: PRESENTATION VARIATIONS

Preschool: Awareness activities for this age group require careful consideration of the maturity of the group, the size of the group, and their attention span. The pre-school child presents differently at each age level between 3 and 5 years. For this age group the development of shared interests is the primary focus for awareness activities. Step 4 -7 outlined in Section 2 would be appropriate for this group. Awareness for this age group is accomplished with little steps either in small groups or in larger group activities. Other topics might include similarities and differences, things friends do together, likes and dislikes, and how friends can be a helper. Developmentally as a whole this age group is just learning and refining social relationship skills, thus learning to share, take turns and thinking about another person is part of the curriculum for the typically developing child. Incidental and experiential awareness activities are often most effective with this age group as describe in the following example.

Mario is four years old and attends a Cooperative Preschool three days a week. At two years of age he was diagnosed with Autistic Disorder. In spite of intensive intervention Mario had not developed spoken language. He is responsive to a picture exchange system. Although the children at the preschool are nice to Mario there is little to no reciprocal interaction due in part to his lack of spoken language. One day during snack Mario was working with an individual aide using his communication book to request his snack items. A curious student asked why Mario could not talk. The student was told that Mario hadn't learned how to talk yet so he used pictures instead. In a few minutes the peer was taught how to communicate with Mario. This activity resulted in more social exchanges as all the other children wanted to learn how to talk with Mario using pictures.

Kindergarten: The kindergarten age group is more able to participate in a formal lesson as they are beginning to demonstrate a greater understanding of perspective. The activity still must be kept short. The teacher may provide follow-up activities which are incorporated into the curriculum, such as doing a bar graph of all the students likes as identified in Step 4. To sustain the student's attention visualization activities may be incorporated. For instance as mentioned in Step 1, each student is given an imaginary present of a new thinking cap. The facilitator pretends to pass out gift boxes. When each student and staff has a gift box the facilitator pretends to open her box and bring out the thinking cap. Everyone puts his or her thinking cap on, adjust the cap and the lesson begins. It is often helpful with this age group to have the focus student's mother and/or father participate in the presentation. The parents may bring baby pictures and family pictures which provides the beginning of a shared history. The following example demonstrates how a mother helped the facilitator introduce her son to his new kindergarten classmates.

>Chuck was going to start kindergarten at his neighborhood school. He was going to be attending school with his siblings now. Everyone was excited but also a little apprehensive since Chuck has Autism and had not attended a general education classroom on a full-time basis. He had been participating in early intervention programs at home and in special classes since he was diagnosed at age two. He had developed some language, readiness skills and play skills; however his restricted patterns of behavior and sensory issues occasionally caused him to behave in unusual ways. To help his new classmates understand Chuck a little better his Mom wrote a book called, I'm A Lot Like You! (See Appendix B) In this book she talked about his family, his like, what was hard for him, what he did when he was upset, and how his classmates could be helpful friends. There were many wonderful pictures that illustrated how Chuck and his peers were more alike than different. Chuck had a good year in kindergarten and still attends his neighborhood school with friends who understand him.

1st and 2nd Grades: If the student with disabilities has been attending the same school with basically the same group of students the facilitator may opt to omit Steps 1 and 2 from the "What Makes School Great?" activity. The activity could begin with Step 3 and a focus on friendship. Students in this age group can participate in activities that last a little longer.

Based on the expected outcomes the facilitator might try a different introductory activity. The introduction might focus on similarities and difference. The activity could begin with things that an individual is born with, such as eye color or hair color. This could be compared to things that are acquired, such as likes and dislikes. Step 3 can then expand to cover accepting individual difference.

With this age group books on friendship might also be incorporated into the activity either as an introduction or as a follow-up with the classroom teacher. There are many books listed for this and other age groups in the Resources at the end of this chapter. The following example describes how, after reading a book, the children were lead in an activity to write their own book.

Molly attends first grade at her neighborhood school. She had been diagnosed with High Functioning Autism in preschool. She has good verbal skills, is an excellent decoder and has great rote memory for facts. Her restricted patterns of behavior and resistance to change cause her a great deal of difficult interacting with her peers. She wants to have friends but is often too assertive and demanding, thus causing her peers to stay away from her. Molly's parents felt that her classmates needed to understand the underlying reasons for Molly's behavior and gave permission for her disability of Autism to be presented. They did not think that Molly was ready for this type of presentation so they kept her home the morning of the presentation. Beverly Bishop's book entitled, *My Friend with Autism* (2002) was used to introduce the activity. This book focuses on things that are easy for children with autism and things that are difficult. The book concludes with ways children with autism can be helped.

After reading this book the children identified Molly's strength, what was hard for her, and finally what they could do as friends to help her. The student's ideas were listed on the board. They were then give a 3 page booklet to write a story about Molly starting the story with her strengths, what her Autism made hard for her, and finally what they were going to do to help her. (See Appendix C) They illustrated their pages and shared them with the facilitator on a return visit. This and on-going awareness activities have supported Molly and her classmates as they grow to understand each other. Molly continues to attend her neighborhood school and make improvements in all areas.

3rd – 5th Grades (Disability Specific): If the student is new to the school all steps may be followed until Step 5. At Step 5 the idea that certain things are difficult for the focus student may be introduced. The students may be asked to identify what they have observed. The disability may be described without actually naming it or the disability may be named. If the disability is named it should be done is a neutral manner explaining that this is just the way the focus student was born. The comparison of being born with specific eye and hair color can be made. If the focus student is present he or she may want to make a comment. It is important to point out that the disability is not contagious. Follow-up activities may include reading disability specific books or watching movies. General educators may also want to infuse the awareness into writing assignments, art, PE, literature, and social studies.

If the student has been attending the same school for many years and his or her disability has been named, the steps many be altered to meet the current learning needs of the class. The class may start at Step 4 and identify the strengths, interest and what is hard for the focus student that they have observed. A disability specific book may be read. A follow-up activity for the upper grades might be to write their own awareness book specific to the focus student they know or develop plans for how they can help the focus student improve in the areas that are difficult for him/her. The following example is from a third grade classroom.

Wes is a third grade student who had been attending the same school since Kindergarten. Although Wes has many skills, his inability to self-regulate his emotional responses in a general education setting prevented him from full time placement in general education. When the school staff was preparing to begin to include Wes more in the general education classroom the team decided that awareness activities were necessary for the typical peers. Because Wes had been attending a Special Day Classroom the team (including the parents) decided that it was important for his classmates to understand Autism and how this affected Wes' behavior, learning, communication, and social responses. His third grade teacher decided to follow up after the awareness activity with an expository writing assignment for his class. His third grade class developed the following essay with each student creating an illustration to represent the focus student in class.

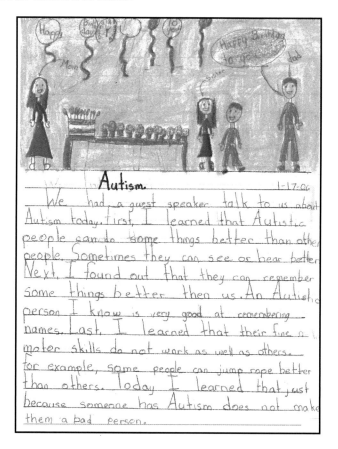

6th – 12th Grades: Students in these grades are usually able to take a more in-depth look at what makes school great for themselves and others. If there is a need to introduce a new student to a school, all the steps may be followed at a sophistication level appropriate to the grade. Activities such as The Sixth Sense (Gray 2002) may be added in place of Step 1 and 2, to assist the students in developing a better understanding of the causes of the social difficulties experienced especially by students with an Autism Spectrum Disorder or other social cognitive disabilities. More detailed characteristic of the specific disability may be shared. When discussing Autism Spectrum Disorders the group may be taught the three core deficit areas of socialization, communication and restricted patterns of behavior. The class may be able to identify the focus student's strengths and difficulties under the 3 areas, thus giving the class a more specific picture of how the disability affects the focus student. These older age groups often will develop specific plans for friendship and supports for the current year or for the future. They may also identify growth they have seen over time. This example describes participation at the high school level.

> Jacob was diagnosed with High Functioning Autism in preschool. He entered his neighborhood school in kindergarten. He spent his entire school career in the same school district transitioning through the grades with the same peers. Upon entering a high school, which drew from many districts, his IEP team decided that these new peers should develop an

understanding of Autism and how it affected Jacob's learning and ability to interact socially. Jacob knew he had Autism but he did not dwell on this. He had other things to do like read the dictionary or the encyclopedia and pursue his interest in facts. When Jacob was ask if he would like to participate in a few Autism awareness activities in his class he declined saying, "I already know about Autism, I would like to go and read."

In the beginning of Jacob's freshman, sophomore, and juniors years in high school awareness activities were held in each of his six classes. Jacob was accepted by his peers and respected for his strengths and supported in his areas of difficulty. In the beginning of Jacob's senior year it was decided that the awareness activities were no longer needed. Although Jacob still required adult assistance in certain areas of academic and social life on campus he was a member of the clubs and appreciated on campus for his strengths.

Discussing Problem Behaviors across the Age Groups:
When the goal of the activity is to discuss problem behaviors, it is usually best if the focus student is not present. The group typically feels more comfortable identifying their concerns. The activity may start with Step 3. Step 4 may be modified to ask, "What would it be like if your friend is not being a friend?" Step 5, the facilitator might ask if the students or teacher have noticed any problems that the

focus student may have. If disability specific information is to be provided it could be provided at this point. If no specific disability information is to be given, then as the problems are identified the facilitator may ask why they think the student is doing that behavior and how they think a friend might help the focus student with the problems. Strategies that may be provided to add to the student's ideas include:

- Identify the replacement behavior so all the students know the goal.
- Give the typical students specific words to say or actions to take.
- Role play interaction and methods for support.
- Make a list of friendship ideas for the focus student to learn.
- Draw a picture of their ideas and make a class book.
- Set up a system of reinforcement for demonstration good friendship skills for all members of the class.
- Create videos or photo albums that show great friendship behavior.

Mickey was diagnosed with Asperger Syndrome in third grade. Mickey has a history of uncooperative behavior. Occasionally, he would growl or shake his fist at peers or staff if he was angry. The IEP team felt is was very important to explain to Mickey's peers why his social skills were not typical for his age. What Makes School Great? and The Sixth Sense activities where blended and a frank discussion of the problem behaviors and strategies to assist Mickey were discussed with Mickey out of the classroom. Follow up sessions included Mickey and involved activities to help the class identify shared interest so that Mickey and his peers could begin to learn to interact. Small social groups were set up during recess and lunch to facilitate social interaction. Adult facilitation was required to build relationships.

SECTION 4: CASE STUDIES

High Functioning Autism: Evan is a seventh grade student on a Middle School Campus in the same school district that he has attended since kindergarten. Evan was diagnosed with Autistic Disorder at 24 months of age. Evan's language was delayed, however with speech therapy his verbal skills developed. He appeared to have normal cognition. His greatest areas of difficulty were his extreme rigidity for routines and sensory integration issues. He attended an inclusion preschool class that served students with Individual Educational Programs and typically developing peers. This class was taught by a special educator. Due to his difficult patterns of behavior, when he transitioned to public school, he was placed in a Special Day Class with some mainstreaming into Kindergarten. His parents requested a full time placement in a general education classroom for first grade. Although he was ranked number one student in reading decoding in his class, he continued to have significant difficulty with basic student behaviors and with social interactions. Evan required many supports to be successful in the general education setting including additional staff support, environmental, and academic accommodations.

Evan's ability awareness activities began, when he entered his new school at first grade. Evan was no longer attending his neighborhood school and neither the staff nor students knew him. Because Evan was being introduced to the campus the first awareness activity was "What Makes School Great?" FRIENDS! Evan was always present during the activities. As a younger student Evan participated on a limited basis and basically was in the class, but not attending unless something caught his attention. Because his patterns of behavior were significantly different from his peers his classmates were told about Autism and how it affected Evan. Each year variations of "What Makes School Great? FRIENDS!" were presented to his classmates. His peers, now friends, have been instrumental in making Evan's learning environment the best it can be.

When Evan was in fifth grade he became a more active participant in the back to school awareness activity for two reasons. First, he had learned appropriate student behaviors and social skills from his peers and staff. Second, the activity was presented using a visual tool, the Venn diagram, which Evan used consistently in his school work. This group of fifth grade students acknowledged both Evan's strengths and weakness saying, "That's just Evan." The outcome of the fifth grade awareness activity was to focus on the new skills Evan would need when he transition with his class to middle school. The class was confident that the transition to middle school would be a success because they would be with him to provide friendship and support as needed. The students were correct and the transition to middle school was a success.

Awareness activities continue to be a part of Evan's school year. The focus now is not on getting to know Evan but more about how to help him meet the ever change academic and social demands. His friends help him naturally throughout the day by volunteering their support. There is a weekly "Lunch Bunch" that is comprised of boys and girls who have gone to school with him since elementary school. Evan has his friendship files and loves to hang out with his friends and take their pictures for his scrapbooks.

Awareness activities along with consistent ongoing proximity, shared interests, and history create positive relationship and provide a solid foundation for friendships.

Classic Autism/Non-verbal: Frank is currently a fourth grade student who is receiving his primary services in a Special Day Class for students with mild – moderate disabilities. Frank was diagnosed with Autism prior to 36 months of age. He was not verbal. Frank participated in a 40 hour a week home program and at age four he attended a private preschool with a tutor. In both his preschool setting and his kindergarten class his peers were provided with awareness activities. At the preschool level they were informal and experiential with a focus on teaching the peers to be a communicative partner with Frank's picture communication system. Frank transitioned to his neighborhood school for kindergarten. "What Makes School Great?" FRIENDS!

was used with a focus on Frank's use of pictures to communicate. The peers learned the system and provided many opportunities for practice. Frank transitioned to a Special Day Class for first grade. Frank's family wanted to ensure that he had opportunity to interact daily in a meaningful way with typical peers. Again the "What Makes School Great?" FRIENDS! activity was used to establish an understanding of Frank's needs. Frank did not participate in these activities, as the activities did not hold much interest for him. Two of Frank's favorite activities were running and playing with balls. The students were asked to think about Frank's interests and activities and identify something that would be fun for him to do at recess. The students decided on soccer, but then realized that the rules would be too hard for him to learn and that the game moved too fast. The group identified running and kicking with a group as something they could teach Frank that would be fun for everyone.

Everyone in the class signed up to be part of Frank's Fun Friends at recess group. There were four groups with five students in each group. The students met Frank and a staff at the beginning of recess and played the modified soccer game that the students developed. At the end of the year the class evaluated Frank's progress and listed all the skills he had learned beside kicking and running. The entire group and Frank were proud of themselves and ready to plan for the next year.

The next year there were two classes that participated in Frank's program. These classes continued the recess skills and asked if Frank could come to their classes for other activities and all the field trips. Although Frank did not participate in academic activities he was definitely a member of the general education class with a circle of friends who greeted him at school and in the community.

Asperger Syndrome: Clark was diagnosed with hyperlexia in preschool. Clark was very verbal and academically advanced for his age. He had difficulty with social interactions, transitions, and a rigid adherence to routines. It was always assumed that given his high cognitive skills that his other difficulties would correct themselves. The opposite seemed to be true. During the primary grades Clark had difficulty making and keeping friends. He would frequently be disruptive in class. In the fourth grade he was diagnosed with Asperger Syndrome. His parents requested that the diagnosis be kept confidential. When Clark transitioned to middle school he also moved to a new school district.

The school welcomed Clark; however the staff was unfamiliar with the needs of a student with Asperger Syndrome. Clark did not know a single student on campus and his social difficulties were magnified in the eyes of peers who did not understand some of his unconventional responses to social situations. It was decided that everyone on campus needed awareness activities.

Clark's family decided that before other people could learn about how Asperger Syndrome affected Clark that Clark needed to understand that there was a reason for his social difficulties at school. Therefore, the first awareness activity was with Clark. His parent requested assistance from an Autism Specialist who had worked with Clark in a social skills group and had a rapport with him. During a home visit, Asperger Syndrome was discussed in general as it related to students who had difficulty with social skills. The book *Finding Out about Asperger Syndrome, High Functioning Autism and PDD* (Gerland,1997) was shared with Clark and his family. Clark thought about the information that had been shared and then said, "Is that why sounds are always so loud in my ears?" From that time on Clark learned as much as he could about Asperger Syndrome.

General awareness activities were held with his classmates as Clark was not ready to disclose that he had Asperger Syndrome. He was comfortable talking with his teachers and shared information with them at his IEP meetings. He now knew why he had difficulty making friends and was motivated to work actively on friendship skills. One day he said, "Thinking about how to be a friend is exhausting."

Clark is in high school and building friendships around shared interests. He has even helped younger children with ASD understand that there are lots of "cool" things you can do when you have ASD and that real friends are OK with you just the way you are.

REFERENCES

Bartak, L., and Rutter, M. Special education treatment of autistic children: A comparative study: I. Design of study and characteristics of units. *Journal of Child Psychology and Psychiatry and Allied Disciplines*. 14(3):161-178, 1973.

Danko, C.D., Lawry, J. and Strain, P.S. *Social Skills Interventions Manual Packet.* Pittsburgh, PA: St. Peters Child Development Center, 1998 unpublished.

Gray, C. *The Sixth Sense II.* Arlington, TX: Future Horizons, Inc. 2002.www.FutureHorizons-autism.com

Gerland, G. *Finding Out about Asperger Syndrome, High Functioning Autism and PDD.* London, England: Jessica Kingsley Publishers, 1997.

Kinny, J. and Fischer, D. *Co-Teaching Students with Autism K-5.* Verona, WI: IEP Resources, 2001. www.attainmentcompany.com

National Research Council. *Educating Children with Autism.* Washington DC: National Academy Press, 2001.

Ozonoff, S., Rogers, S., and Hendren, R. *Autism Spectrum Disorders: A Research for Practitioners.* London, England: American Psychiatric Publishing, 2003.

Wolfberg, P. *Peer Play and the Autism Spectrum.* Shawnee Mission, KS: Autism Aspergers Publishing Company, 2003. www.asperger.net

RESOURCES

Ability Awareness Book List for Young to Elementary Age Children

Bishop, B. *My Friend with Autism.* Arlington, TX: Future Horizons, Inc. 2002. www.FutureHorizons-autism.com

Edwards, A. *Taking Autism to School.* Hawthorn, NY: JayJo Books, 2001.

Elder, J. *Different Like Me: My Book of Autism Heroes.* London, England: Jessica Kingsley Publishing, 2006. www.jkp.com

Katz, I. and Ritvo, E. *Joey and Sam.* Northridge CA: Real Life Story Books, 1993.

Larson, E. M. *I Am Utterly Unique: Celebrating the Strengths of Children with Asperger Syndrome and High Functioning Autism.* Shawnee Mission, KS: Autism Aspergers Publishing Company, 2006. www.asperger.net

Lear, L. *Ian's Walk: A Story about Autism.* Morton Grove, Illinois: Albert Whitman & Company, 1998.

Lowell, J. and Tuchel, T. *My Best Friend Will.* Shawnee Mission, KS: Autism Aspergers Publishing Company, 2005. www.asperger.net

Luchsinger, D. and Olson, J. *Playing by the Rules: A Story about Autism.* Bethesda, MD: Woodbine House, 2007.

Maguire, A. *Special People Special Ways.* Arlington, TX: Future Horizons Inc., 2000. www.FutureHorizons-autism.com

Messner, A. W. *Captain Tommy*. Arlington, TX: Future Horizons, Inc., 1996. www.FutureHorizons-autism.com

Murrell, D. *Tobin Makes Friends*. Arlington, TX: Future Horizons, Inc., 2002. www.FutureHorizons-autism.com

Sabin, E. *The Autism Acceptance Book*. Printed in China: Watering Can Press, 2006. www.wateringcanpress.com

Simmons, K. *Little Rainman: Autism through the Eyes of a Child*. Arlington, TX: Future Horizons, Inc., 2000. www.FutureHorizons-autism.com

Thompson, M. *Andy and his Yellow Frisbee*. Bethesda, MD: Woodbine House, 1996.

Twachtman-Cullen, D. *Trevor Trevor*. Higganum, CT: Starfish Press, 1998. www.starfishpress.com

Book List for Upper Elementary to Adolescences

Gagnon, E. & Smith-Myles, B. *This is Asperger Syndrome*. London, England: Jessica Kingsley Publishers, 1999. www.jkp.com.

Hall, K. *Asperger Syndrome: The Universe and Everything*. London, England: Jessica Kingsley Publishers, 2001.

Hoopman, K. *Blue Bottle Mystery: An Asperger Adventure*. London, England: Jessica Kingsley Publishers, 2000. www.jkp.com.

Hoopman, K. *Lace and the Lacemaker: An Asperger Adventure*. London, England: Jessica Kingsley Publishers, 2001. www.jkp.com.

Jackson, L. *Freaks, Geeks & Asperger Syndrome: A User Guide to Adolescence*. London, England: Jessica Kingsley Publishing, 2002. www.jkp.com.

Keating-Velasco, J. L. *A is for Autism, F is for Friend.* Shawnee Mission, KS: Autism Aspergers Publishing Company, 2007. www.asperger.net

Lord, C. *Rules.* New York, NY: Scholastic, 2006.

Orgaz, N. *Buster and the Amazing Daisy: Adventures with Asperger Syndrome.* Washington DC and London, England: Jessica Kingsley Publishers, 2002. www.jkp.com.

Schnurr, R. *Asperger's Huh?* Arlington, TX: Future Horizons, Inc., 1999. www.FutureHorizons-autism.com

Welton, J. *Can I tell you about Asperger Syndrome? A guide for friends and family.* Washington DC and London, England: Jessica Kingsley Publishers, 2004. www.jkp.com.

Book List for Adults

Attwood, T. *Why does Chris do that?* Shawnee Mission, KS: Autism Aspergers Publishing Company,1993. www.asperger.net

Burrows, E. L. and Wagner, S. J. *Understanding Asperger's Syndrome, Fast Facts: A Guide for Teachers and Educators to Address the Needs of the Student.* Arlington, TX: Future Horizons, Inc., 2004. www.FutureHorizons-autism.com

Grandin, T. *Emergence Labeled Autistic.* Navato, CA: Warner Books, 1986.

Grandin, T. *Thinking in Pictures and Other Reports from my Life with Autism.* New York, NY: Vintage Books, 1996.

Holliday Willey, L. *Pretending to be Normal.* Washington DC and London, England: Jessica Kingsley Publishers, 1999. www. jkp.com.

Holliday Willey, L. *Asperger's in the Family: Redefining Normal.* London, England: Jessica Kingsley Publishers, 2001. www.jkp.com.

Ledgin, N. *Asperger's and Self-Esteem: Insight and Hope Through Famous Role Models.* Arlington, TX: Future Horizons, Inc., 2002. www.FutureHorizons-autism.com

Newport, J. *Your Life is Not a Label: A Guide to Living Fully with Autism and Asperger Syndrome.* Arlington, TX: Future Horizons, Inc., 2001. www.FutureHorizons-autism.com

Newport, J., Newport, M., and Dodd, J. *Mozart and the Whale: An Asperger's Love Story.* New York, NY: Simon and Schuster, 2007.

Robison, J. E. *Look Me in the Eye.* New York, NY: Three Rivers Press, 2007.

Shore, S. *Beyond the Wall: Personal Experiences with Autism and Asperger Syndrome.* Shawnee Mission, KS: Autism Aspergers Publishing Company, 2003. www.asperger.net

Tammet, D. *Born on a Blue Day A Memoir: Inside the Extraordinary Mind of an Autistic Savant.* Great Britain: Free Press, 2007.

Williams, D. *Nobody, Nowhere: The Extraordinary Autobiography of An Autistic.* New York, NY: Times Books, 1992.

Williams, D. *Somebody, Somewhere: Breaking Free from the World of Autism.* New York, NY: Three River Press, 1994.

Williams, D. *Like Color to the Blind: Soul Searching and Soul Finding.* New York, NY: Times Books, 1996.

Book List for Self-Awareness

Faherty, C. *Asperger's: What Does It Mean to Me?* Arlington, TX: Future Horizons, Inc. 2000. www.FutureHorizons-autism.com

Korin, E.S. *Asperger Syndrome an Owner's Manual: What You, Your Parents and Your Teachers Needs to Know.* Shawnee Mission, KS: Autism Asperger Publishing Company, 2006.

Korin, E.S. *Asperger Syndrome an Owner's Manual for Older Adolescents and Adults: What You, Your Parents and Friends, and Your Employer, Needs to Know.* Shawnee Mission, KS: Autism Asperger Publishing Company, 2007.

Websites

The Autism Society of Delaware: This organization is comprised family members and friends of people with autism, and professionals who work in the autism field. Their mission is to improve the lives of people with autism and their families. They educate, advocate and raise public awareness in order to promote lifelong opportunity and acceptance for people with autism in their communities. The website listed below is for kids only and is designed to help children understand ASD.

http://www.delautism.org/kids_only.htm

The TEACCH Program: A Division of the Department of Psychiatry mission is to enable individuals with autism to function as meaningfully and as independently as possible in the community; to provide exemplary services throughout North Carolina to individuals with autism and their families and those who serve and support them. As a member of the University community, to generate knowledge; to integrate clinical services with relevant theory and research; and to disseminate information about theory, practice, and research on autism through training and publications locally, nationally and internationally. The following link on their website provides generic and specific awareness activities.

http://teacch.com/understandingfriends.html

APPENDIX A
THE SCHOOL PARTICIPATION CHECKLIST

LONGITUDINAL DATA AND TRENDS

Between 2000 and 2005 there were 77 students with an Autism Spectrum Disorder assessed using the School Participation Checklist (SPC). The grade level of the 77 students ranged from preschool through 8th grade. These students attended various schools in different school districts in the same county.

The assessment of many students over several years has demonstrated the value of systematically tracking a focus student in basic student behaviors. The results have also given educators guidance in developing instructional programs to address student behavior skills that many often think are learned incidentally, just by being in proximity of average students.

General educators were asked to select an "average" student. This average student was neither the best nor the most challenging student, but was the best representative of the average student of the same age and gender as the student with special needs who was being assessed. The general educator then completed a School Participation Checklist (SPC) on that average student. The purpose of completing the SPC on the average student is to provide the average criteria for performance of student behavior in a specific setting and grade.

The use of the SPC over a five year period revealed the following trends, which could be considered an informal standardization of the checklist. The patterns of responses for the "average" school age student are as follows:

- The majority of general educator's total score across all the areas ranged from 0 to 6 points out of 18 points possible, for school age students from kindergarten to 8th grade. The lower the point score indicates more appropriate student behavior and less need for intervention.

- Students usually only scored outside the 0-6 range when they were very young, preschool or kindergarten students, or had other issues such as AD/HD.

- The average student often showed a need for some additional support in the areas of patterns of behavior and attending.

- The strongest areas for the average student were communication and social skills.

The "focus" student for all assessments during the 5 year period was a student with an Autism Spectrum Disorder (ASD), who had been identified for assessment of his/her student behaviors in a general education classroom. For focus students who were enrolled in the inclusive setting the general educator completed the SPC on the focus student, after completing the SPC on the average student. If the focus student had not yet been placed in the general education setting then the special educator completed the SPC on the focus student in preparation for the student to move to the general education setting.

Patterns for the focus student assessed by general educators revealed the following trends:

- There is an overall uneven pattern of skills.

- Social Skills are typically the most significantly challenged area.

- Given systematic comprehensive early intervention the most growth is noted during the early learning years between preschool and 1st grade.

- Beginning in 2nd or 3rd grade the focus student begins to stabilize at an average score of 7 to 9 out of 18 possible points, depending on the developmental level of the student.

  - It is hypothesized that this occurs because the skills required for school participation are becoming more abstract and subtle. When the skills required become more abstract the focus student again requires more instruction. Thus, rather than moving a skill from learning to mastery to the generalized level, the focus student stays at the learning level because the scope of the skills required have changed from the previous year.

- When comparing the scores of a Special Educator to a General Educator's scores it is noted that a Special Educator usually scores the focus student as more skillful than the General Educator.

  - It is hypothesized that this occurs because of the significant accommodation and modification in place for the student environmentally, socially, and academically within a Special Day Class.

Figure A.4 provides a comparison of the average students and the focus students assessed over a 5 year period. All the focus students reported in the sample were diagnosed with an Autism Spectrum Disorder. Table A.1 shows that 52% of the average students required10% or less support from the teacher to perform appropriate student behaviors, while only 1% of the focus students scored in this range. The totals indicate that 87% of the average students required additional support 30% of the time or less, whereas only 12% of the focus students functioned at this level.

Percentage of Time Requiring Support

	10%	20%	30%	Totals
Average Student	52%	19%	16%	87%
Focus Student	1%	3%	8%	12%

Figure A.1

Figures A.2 and A.3 break the data down further and indicate the significant need that the focus student has for instruction and support in basic behaviors to perform as a student in an inclusive setting. The overall trends revealed by this data indicate that 87% of the "average" students require additional support or intervention from the teacher 30% or less of the time, whereas 88% of the "focus students" required supports and interventions 40 – 100% of the time.

Percentage of Time Requiring Support

	40%	50%	60%	Totals
Average Student	7%	5%	>1%	12%
Focus Student	12%	20%	21%	53%

Figure A.2

Percentage of Time Requiring Support

	70%	80%	90%	100%	Totals
Average Student	>1%	0%	0%	0%	>1%
Focus Student	19%	11%	3%	2%	35%

Figure A.3

It can be concluded from this data that students with special needs, especially those with an Autism Spectrum Disorder require additional supports and interventions just to perform appropriate student behaviors in a general education setting. The data from the SPC indicates that appropriate student behaviors, the keys to successful learning, can be identified and addressed in a systematic way.

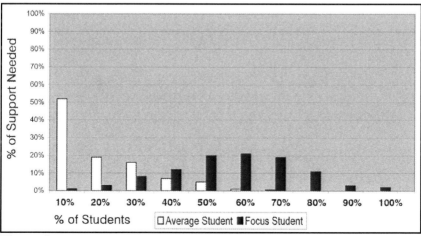

Figure A.4

APPENDIX B

IDEAS FOR PARENTS OR PROFESSIONALS TO CREATE AND USE A PERSONAL AWARENESS BOOK

I'm A Lot Like You!

This outline may be used as presented or varied to meet the individual needs of the child and the situation. The original book was designed to have one or more photographs per page. The book may be photocopies or presented as an album or scrapbook. The book may be read straight through or comments from the class can be solicited as the book is read to the average peers.

Page 1.   My name is _____.
Page 2.   I am _____ years old.
           I live with my _____.
           I'm going to be in your class very soon.
Page 3.   I am just like you in lots of ways.
           Some of my favorite things to eat are _____.
           But, I really love _____.
Page 4.   We might be alike in other ways too.
           I like _____.
Page 5.   I also like _____.
Page 6.   Sometimes I need extra help to do the things I like.
           I also need a little more help at school. So, a helper will be with me most of the time.
           It's hard to understand when people talk to me because I learn differently than you.
Page 7.   If I get frustrated or feel scared or tired, I might scrunch up my face, or play with my hands, or even cry.
           But, I get really upset if you cry because it makes me so sad I don't know what to do.
Page 8.   If I need to be alone to make myself feel better, I might look for something soft to play with or find a pretty plant to pick leave and flowers from. I might even hum to myself.
Page 9.   But don't worry, I'll be just fine!
Page 10.   Don't forget! There are lots of things I can do and want to do just like you.
Page 11.   I can't wait to be in your class! See you soon.

APPENDIX C
IDEAS FOR CHILDREN TO WRITE A BOOK

I Have a Friend with Autism

A follow-up activity for children who have participated in a disability specific awareness activity about a classmate is to write a book. This format was originally designed for elementary age students; however the concept could be expanded upon to allow older students to do a similar writing activity. The following outline provides the details included on each page of the book.

Cover Page: Title "I Have a Friend with Autism"

Written and Illustrated by _____.

Page1: I have a friend with Autism.

I think that my friend is good at _____.

Page 2: Autism makes some things hard for my friend to do.

I think it is hard for my friends to

_____.

Page 3: I can be a helpful friend when I _____.

An activity book with this format is available at
www.abtaproducts.com

Companion CD INDEX
R.E.A.D.Y. for Inclusion Companion CD
FORM Templates and Reproducible Handouts
Listed by Chapters

Chapter 1
Getting R.E.A.D.Y. for Inclusion with a Shared Vision

1. FORM: <u>INCLUSIVE EDUCATION: Training & Self confidence Self Evaluation Survey</u>
   READY-C1-01.pdf
   a. SAMPLE: INCLUSIVE EDUCATION: Training & Self confidence Self Evaluation Survey
      READY-C1-01a.pdf
   b. SAMPLE: Quantifiable Data Shown as Percentage from Self Evaluation with Instructions for scorer
      READY-C1-01b.pdf

2. FORM: <u>Inclusive Education: Training and Competence Self Evaluation Summary of Data</u>
   READY-C1-02.pdf
   a. SAMPLE: Inclusive Education: Training and Competence Self Evaluation Summary of Data
      READY -C1-02a.pdf
   b. SUBMISSION FORM: Inclusive Education: Training and Competence Self Evaluation Summary of Data
      READY-C1-02b.pdf

Chapter 2
R. - Readiness of Student Behavior

1. FORM Package: <u>The School Participation Checklist</u>
   READY-C2-01-SPC-FORMS.pdf
   SPC-Instructions.pdf
   SPC-StereotypedBehavior.pdf
   SPC-FORM-PK-3.pdf
   SPC-FORM-4-8.pdf
   SPC-FORM-9-12.pdf
   SPC-ANALYSIS-PK-3.pdf
   SPC-ANALYSIS-4-8.pdf
   SPC-ANALYSIS-9-12.pdf
   SPC-AccomMod.pdf
   SPC-SCORE-FORM.pdf
   SPC-SAMPLE-FORM.pdf
   SPC-SAMPLE-ANALYSIS.pdf
   SPC-SAMPLE-SCORE-FORM.pdf

2. FILL IN FORM Package: <u>The School Participation Checklist</u>
    READY-C2-02-SPC-FORMS-FILL-IN.pdf

    SPC-Instructions.pdf

    SPC-StereotypedBehavior.pdf

    SPC-FORM-PK-3-FI.pdf

    SPC-FORM-4-8-FI.pdf

    SPC-FORM-9-12-FI.pdf

    SPC-ANALYSIS-PK-3-FI.pdf

    SPC-ANALYSIS-4-8-FI.pdf

    SPC-ANALYSIS-9-12-FI.pdf

    SPC-AccomMod-FI.pdf

    SPC-SCORE-FORM-FI.pdf

    SPC-SAMPLE-FORM.pdf

    SPC-SAMPLE-ANALYSIS.pdf
    SPC-SAMPLE-SCORE-FORM.pdf

3. FORM Package: The SPC for Multiple Teachers
    READY-C2-03-SPC-FORMS-MULTI.pdf

    SPC-02Teachers.pdf

    SPC-03Teachers.pdf

    SPC-04Teachers.pdf

    SPC-05Teachers.pdf

4. FILL IN FORM Package: The SPC Form Sets by Grades
    READY-C2-04-SPC-FORM-SETS-FILL-IN.pdf

    SPC-PK-3-FormSET-FI.pdf

    SPC-4-8-FormSET-FI.pdf
    SPC-9-12-FormSET-FI.pdf

Chapter 3
E. - Environment for Instruction
1. FORM: The V.E.S.T.
    READY-C3-01.pdf

Chapter 4
A. - Accommodating for Academic and Learning Differences
1. FORM: <u>Accommodation and Modification Planning Form</u>
    READY-C4-01.pdf

    a. FILL IN FORM: <u>Accommodation and Modification Planning Form</u>
        READY-C4-01a.pdf

2. FORM: R.E.A.D.Y. MATRIX for Accommodation and Modification
    READY-C4-02.pdf
    a. SAMPLE: R.E.A.D.Y. MATRIX for Accommodation and
        Modification
        READY-C4-02a.pdf
    b. FILL IN FORM: R.E.A.D.Y. MATRIX for Accommodation
        and Modification
        READY-C4-02b.pdf

2. FORM: Accommodation and Modification Classroom Data
    Collection Form
    READY-C4-03.pdf
    a. SAMPLE: Accommodation and Modification Classroom
        Data Collection Form
        READY-C4-3a.pdf
    b. FILL IN: Accommodation and Modification Classroom
        Data Collection Form
        READY-C4-3b.pdf

Chapter 5
D. - Determining Levels of Support
1. FORM Package: Individual Support Assessment (3 Areas of Need)
    READY-C5-01.pdf
    a. FORM: Student Needs Rubric
        READY-C5-01a.pdf
    b. FILL IN FORM: Student Needs Rubric
        READY-C5-01b.pdf
    c. FORM: Referral for Supplementary Staff Support
        READY-C5-01c.pdf
    d. FILL IN FORM: Referral for Supplementary Staff Support
        READY-C5-01d.pdf
    e. FORM: Referral for Supplementary Staff Support: Part 2 & 3
        Analysis of IEP Goals Form (Optional Use)
        READY-C5-01e.pdf
    f. FILL IN FORM: Referral for Supplementary Staff Support: Part
        2 & 3 Analysis of IEP Goals Form (Optional Use)
        READY-C5-01f.pdf
    g. FORM: Current Staff Support Schedule (3 or 5 areas of Need)
        READY-C5-01g.pdf
    h. FILL IN FORM: Current Staff Support Schedule (3 or 5 areas of
        Need)
        READY-C5-01h.pdf

2. FORM Package: Individual Support Assessment (5 Areas of Need)
   READY-C5-02.pdf
   a.. FORM: Student Needs Rubric
      READY-C5-02a.pdf
   b. FILL IN FORM: Student Needs Rubric
      READY-C5-02b.pdf
   c. FORM: Referral for Supplementary Staff Support
      READY-C5-02c.pdf
   d. FILL IN FORM: Referral for Supplementary Staff Support
      READY-C5-02d.pdf
   e. FORM: Referral for Supplementary Staff Support: Part 2 & 3
      Analysis of IEP Goals Form (Optional Use)
      READY-C5-02e.pdf
   f. FILL IN FORM: Referral for Supplementary Staff Support: Part
      2 & 3 Analysis of IEP Goals Form (Optional Use)
      READY-C5-02f.pdf
   g. FORM: Current Staff Support Schedule (3 or 5 areas of Need)
      READY-C5-02g.pdf
   h. FILL IN FORM: Current Staff Support Schedule (3 or 5 areas of
      Need)
      READY-C5-02h.pdf

3. FORM Package: Staff Responsibilities
   READY-C5-03.pdf
   a. FORM: READY-C5-03a.pdf
   b. SAMPLE: READY-C5-03b.pdf
   c. FORM FILL IN: READY-C5-03c.pdf

4. FORM Package: Classroom Participation Plan
   READY-C5-04.pdf
   a. FORM: READY-C5-04a.pdf
   b. SAMPLE: READY-C5-04b.pdf
   c. FILL IN FORM: READY-C5-04c.pdf

5. FORM Package: R.E.A.D.Y. Matrix for Measurable Annual Goals
   and Classroom Schedule
   READY-C5-05.pdf
   a. FORM: READY-C5-05a.pdf
   b. SAMPLE: READY-C5-05b.pdf
   c. FILL IN FORM: READY-C5-05c.pdf

6. FORM Package: R.E.A.D.Y. Matrix Middle School and High School
READY-C5-06.pdf
   a. FORM: READY-C5-06a.pdf
   b. SAMPLE: READY-C5-06b.pdf
   c. FILL IN FORM: READY-C5-06c.pdf

Chapter 6:
Y. - Your Natural Supports: Peers
1. FORM Package: What Makes School Great? PLANNING CHECKLIST
READY-C6-01.pdf
   a. FORM: READY:06-01a.pdf
   b. SAMPLE:READY:06-01b.pdf
   c. FILL IN FORM: READY:06-01c.pdf